TWAYNE'S WORLD AUTHORS SERIES
A Survey of the World's Literature

Sylvia E. Bowman, Indiana University
GENERAL EDITOR

MEXICO

Luis Dávila, Indiana University
EDITOR

Carlos Pellicer

TWAS 451

Carlos Pellicer

CARLOS PELLICER

By EDWARD J. MULLEN
University of Missouri, Columbia

TWAYNE PUBLISHERS

A DIVISION OF G. K. HALL & CO., BOSTON

Library of Congress Cataloging in Publication Data

Mullen, Edward J   1942–
  Carlos Pellicer.

  (Twayne's world authors series ; TWAS 451 : Mexico)
  Bibliography: p. 165–67.
  Includes index.
  1. Pellicer, Carlos, 1897–   2. Poets, Mexican—
20th century—Biography.
PQ7297.P3Z78   861   [B]   77-1959
ISBN 0-8057-6288-4

For Helen and Kathleen

Contents

About the Author

Preface

Chronology

1. The Historical Background   15
2. The Early Poetry: The Animated Tropics   32
3. *Sacrificial Stone:* The Voice of Social Concern   49
4. A Return to the Simple Life: *Six, Seven Poems*   63
5. The Transplanted Tropics: *One Twenty*   77
6. *Highway:* The Plateau   87
7. On the Road to Maturity   94
8. The Mature Poet: *Subordinations* and *Practice of Flight*   106
9. Recent Poetry   123
10. Final Appraisal   141
     Notes and References   153
     Selected Bibliography   165
     Index   168

About the Author

Edward J. Mullen is currently associate professor of Romance languages at the University of Missouri, Columbia. He was formerly an assistant professor of modern languages at Purdue University. Dr. Mullen received his B.A. from West Virginia Wesleyan College in 1964; he received the M.A. (1965) and Ph.D. (1968) degrees from Northwestern University.

Among Professor Mullen's writings are *La Revista Contemporáneos: Selección y prólogo*, Editorial Anaya, 1972; *Encuentro: Ensayos de la actualidad*, Holt, 1974; *Lecturas Básicas*, Holt, 1976; *Langston Hughes in the Hispanic World and Haiti*, Shoestring (1977); plus some thirty articles in scholarly journals such as *Romance Notes*, *Hispania*, *Comparative Literature Studies*, *Latin American Theatre Review*, *Review*, *Caribe*, and *Caribbean Review*. Dr. Mullen is a member of the American Association of Teachers of Spanish and Portuguese, and the Modern Language Association of America.

Preface

Among the many anomalies which strike the critic of contemporary Spanish-American letters perhaps one of the most intriguing is the problem of the literary reputation of the Mexican poet, Carlos Pellicer. The study of the critical reception of Pellicer's verse is of interest not only to the student of Mexican letters, but also to a much larger audience.[1] It raises a fundamental question for the student of literature: the relationship between the writer and the critic and, more specifically, the influence of academic criticism on a writer's public reception.

Even a casual glance at histories of Spanish-American literature reveals that Pellicer has been almost universally classified as Mexico's most renowned poet. According to Raúl Leiva, "he has been unanimously recognized as the greatest contemporary Mexican poet."[2] Gustavo Sainz wrote in the famed *Revista Sur:* "Carlos Pellicer . . . is at present, if not the best, one of the greatest poets that Mexico has produced."[3] Octavio Paz has been no less enthusiastic in his appraisal of Pellicer: "Pellicer is the richest and most varied of the poets of his generation."[4] Yet in spite of these affirmations, very few in-depth studies of his poetry have been undertaken, and only a few of his poems have been translated.

An examination of the changing attitude toward his poetry reveals a certain trajectory in critical thought which may prove helpful in explaining the modest reception he has been afforded to date. Perhaps the most important factor in studying the relationship of Pellicer with his critics is his somewhat ambivalent relationship to the literary generation *(Contemporáneos)*. The traditional tendency to group Pellicer with such experimental poets as Jaime Torres Bodet, Bernardo Ortiz de Montellano, Xavier Villaurrutia, and José Gorostiza has reinforced the facile concept of Pellicer as a writer devoid of intellectual profundity.

This book's purpose is to make available for the English-reading public a general study of Pellicer's work and to clarify his position in twentieth-century Mexican literature. Since he has been recognized primarily as a poet, this study will focus almost exclusively on that genre. To afford an appreciation of the general trajectory of his work, a chronological approach has been taken.

For poetry published prior to 1961, reference will be made to the *Material poético 1918–1961* (Mexico: Ediciones UNAM) with page numbers in the text. All translations are mine except where otherwise noted.

I wish to express my gratitude to Sr. Carlos Pellicer for allowing me to quote and translate excerpts from his published works. Special thanks are due to other scholars of Mexican literature, above all, Andrew Debicki, Frank Dauster, and George Melnycovich whose earlier explorations have in many ways made this study possible. I am also grateful to my graduate students, especially Patricia Gulmez and Rosanna Desmeules for their thoughtful readings of Sr. Pellicer's verse.

I gratefully acknowledge a grant from the University of Missouri, Columbia Research Council which helped to support this investigation. A very special word of thanks is due to Professor Benjamin Honeycutt who very carefully read this manuscript.

Finally, the author wishes to thank the following authors and publishers for permission to quote from the books listed: Ernst Benn Ltd., for an excerpt from "The Key of Fire," from *Visitor of the Mist*, edited and translated by G. R. Coulthard. Copyright 1950 by Williams and Norgate. Sr. Jorge Carrera Andrade, for an excerpt from "La llave del fuego," from *Edades Poéticas 1922–1956*. Copyright 1958 by Casa de la Culture Ecuatoriane. New Directions Inc., for an excerpt from "Third time," from *Anthology of Contemporary Latin-American Poetry*, by Dudley Fitts. Copyright 1942 by New Directions Publishing Corporation. Reprinted by permission of New Directions Publishing Corporation. E. P. Dutton & Co., Inc., for an excerpt from "Memoires of Iza" and "Wishes," from *New Poetry of Mexico*, selected, with notes, by Octavio Paz, Ali Chumacero, José Emilio Pacheco, and Homer Aridjis. Bilingual edition edited by Mark Strand. Copyright © 1966 by Siglo XXI Editores, S. A.; English translation copyright © 1970 by E. P. Dutton & Co., Inc., and reprinted with their permission. The Grove Press Inc., for an excerpt from the "United Fruit Co.," from *Selected Poems of Pablo Neruda*, translated by Ben Belitt. Copyright 1961 by Groves Press, Inc. Translator's foreword and English texts copyright © 1961 by Ben Belitt. Robert Márquez and

Name," and "Words in the Tropics," from *Man Making Words: Selected Poems of Nicolás Guillén*. Copyright 1972 by University of Massachusetts Press. The Swallow Press, for excerpts from "Aurora," and "Sketches for a Tropical Ode," from *Three Spanish American Poets: Pellicer, Neruda, Andrade*, translated by Lloyd Mallen, Mary and C. V. Wicker, and J. L. Grucci. Copyright 1942 by Swallow and Critchlow.

EDWARD J. MULLEN

University of Missouri, Columbia

Chronology

1899 Carlos Pellicer born November 4, in Villahermosa, Tabasco.
1910 Start of the Mexican Revolution. Porfirio Díaz is overthrown.
1916 First poem published in literary review, *Gladios*.
1917 Writes prologue for *Poemas de Antonio y Manuel Machado*.
1918 Goes to Bogotá as a representative of the Mexican Federation of Students.
1920 Returns to Mexico.
1921 Publishes poetry in Mexican little magazines: *México Moderno*, *El Maestro*, *América*. Publication of *Colores en el mar y otros poemas*.
1922 Named subsecretary in the Department of Fine Arts. Accompanies José Vasconcelos to Brazil.
1924 Publishes *Piedra de sacrificios* and *Seis, Siete poemas*.
1925 *Bolívar*. Receives scholarship from Puig Casauranc, Secretary of Education, to study in Europe. Sails for Marseilles.
1927 *Hora y 20*.
1929 *Camino*.
1930 Imprisoned for political activities related to Vasconcelos' campaign for the presidency.
1937 *Hora de junio*. Attends writers' conference in Valencia, Spain, and meets Juan Ramón Jiménez, Miguel Hernández, and Rafael Alberti there.
1941 *Recinto y otras imágenes* and *Exágones*.
1949 *Subordinaciones*.
1950 *Sonetos*.
1953 Elected to membership in the Mexican Academy of the Language.
1956 *Práctica de vuelo*.
1959 Publishes the official guide to the Museum of Tabasco.
1960 *La pintura mural de la Revolución Mexicana 1921–1960* which contains an introductory essay by Pellicer.
1961 Publishes "He olvidado mi nombre" in Argentine review, *Sur*.
1962 *Material poético 1918–1961* and *Con palabras y fuego*, collected works.

1964 *Teotihuacán y 13 de agosto: Ruina de Tenochtitlán.* Awarded the National Prize for Literature by Mexican government.

1965 Elected President of the Congress of Latin American Writers in Rome.

1968 Publishes "Líneas por el Che Guevara" in *Cuadernos Americanos.*

1969 *Primera antología poética* published by the Fondo de Cultura Económica.

1977 Pellicer dies February 15 in Mexico City.

CHAPTER 1

The Historical Background

I The Literary Period

CARLOS Pellicer was born during a period of dual unrest in Mexico. Profound changes were taking place in both literary and political spheres at the turn of the century which were to have a lasting effect on Mexican culture. In 1910, when Pellicer was just eleven, the Mexican Revolution erupted. One year later, the poet Enrique González Martínez (1871–1952) published his famous "Tuércele el cuello al cisne" ("Twist the Swan's Neck"), which symbolically marks the conclusion of the modernist period in Spanish-American literature.

The Mexican Revolution not only succeeded in ending the dictatorship of Porfirio Díaz (1830–1915), who had held a political and ideological stranglehold on the nation for more than thirty-five years, but it also gave birth to a cycle of political literature which emphasized the depiction of the Mexican experience as opposed to the exotic, art-for-art's sake orientation of the early modernists. The Revolution marked the entrance of sweeping social reforms, such as the land reform tenets of the Constitution of 1917, but it also signaled the collapse of positivism which had become the almost official philosophy of the Díaz regime. Simply stated, positivism held that theology and metaphysics were imperfect modes of cognition, and that the only valid knowledge was that which is based on natural phenomena and can be empirically analyzed. Derived from the theories of the French philosopher, Auguste Comte and the British thinker, Herbert Spencer, positivism was introduced to Mexico by Gabino Barreda (1824–1881), secretary of education under Benito Juárez (1806–1872), who reorganized higher education in Mexico to conform to his positivistic ideology. As Antonio Caso noted, he banished "the study of the humanities, classical culture, and those literary principles of antiquity that . . . have created the most ex-

15

quisite flowers of thought and the highest rewards of the mind."[1]
This rigid scientism with its bias for technical superiority and
economic gain was adroitly manipulated by a group of Díaz' advis-
ers, the *Científicos,* who sought to exploit the political advantages of
this school of thought.

Thus at approximately the same time that the revolutionary
movement was gaining impetus, the literary world saw the decline
of the modernist school and the beginnings of a new direction in
Mexican letters. There is little doubt that this literary phenomenon
had a pervasive effect on all of Hispanic letters. This movement,
which flourished from about 1888 to 1910 or 1916, was headed by
the Nicaraguan poet Rubén Darío and, among others, the Bolivian
Ricardo Jaimes Freyre, the Argentinian Leopoldo Lugones, the
Peruvian Manuel González Prada, the Mexicans Manuel Gutiérrez
Nájera, Amado Nervo, and Enrique González Martínez, the Peruvian José Santos Chocano, and the Uruguayan Julio Herrera y Reissig. Inspired by the themes and techniques of the French parnas-
sians and symbolists, these writers sought to create a pure art
devoid of social comment. Their prose and above all, their poetry,
was highly stylized, refined, and escapist. Arturo Torres Ríoseco
called the movement "a kind of inverted realism," and noted in it a
"constant escape from immediate reality to the ideal aspiration of
life."[2]

While modernism was responsible in large measure for a renovation of the Spanish-American literary scene, by the time of the
Mexican Revolution it was already in a state of decline. The literary
reputations of the leading Mexican modernists, Manuel Gutiérrez
Nájera (1859–1895) and Amado Nervo (1853–1928) were already
being questioned at the time young Pellicer was beginning his student days. The reaction against the intellectual climate of the day
had been initiated as early as 1906 with the publication of the review
Savia Moderna edited by Luis Castillo Ledón and Alfonso Cravioto,
and later by the organization of the *Ateneo de México* (Atheneum of
Mexico) in 1909. The principal members of the group were José
Vasconcelos (1881–1959), Antonio Caso (1883–1940), Alfonso Reyes
(1889–1959), and the Dominican Pedro Henríquez Ureña (1884–
1946). These men, who were primarily of philosophical bent, shared
a common interest in reorganizing Mexican education and opposing
the rigid positivism of the day with a humanistic spirit of alert intellectual curiosity. As Martin Stabb has observed, "The writers of the

Ateneo were striving to give man a chance to act as a free agent, to act creatively and disinterestedly."[3]

The impact of the *Ateneo* on Pellicer and the generation of writers to which he belonged cannot be overstated. Although by and large the members of the group were not poets, they did contribute substantially to the intellectual information of the generation of Mexican writers known as the *Contemporáneos* ("Contemporaries"), a group to which Pellicer was intimately related. As the Mexican poet Jaime Torres Bodet, a fellow member of the *Contemporáneos*, has stated: "It would be unjust not to recognize what González Martínez' example of intellectual probity, the energetic lessons of José Vasconcelos, and the subtle curiosity of Alfonso Reyes meant to the youngest members. More than their direct influence, what we received from them was the message of the literary and philosophic world in which they were shaping their own conquests."[4]

To complete the picture of the period during which Pellicer emerged as a young poet, attention should be called to the importance of two poets loosely associated with the *Ateneo:* Enrique González Martínez, to whom we have already referred, and Ramón López Velarde (1888–1921). The impact of González Martínez has been attested to by Xavier Villaurrutia, who called him "the supreme and almost only god of our poetry,"[5] and Jaime Torres Bodet, who confessed that "The intelligence of Antonio Caso was most evident in the classroom, but the talent and sensitivity of González Martínez was exchanged by everyone in conversation."[6] The author of carefully wrought, serious verse, his dedication to his art encouraged the younger Mexican poets to avoid the technical excesses of modernism. Frank Dauster aptly summed it up when he said: "González Martínez' true importance as a model lies in his singular devotion to poetry, his insistence on total commitment."[7]

The influence of López Velarde and of the almost forgotten figure of José Juan Tablada (1871–1945) was probably of even more consequence in the development of modern Mexican poetry than that of González Martínez. López Velarde's verse, with its emphasis on the depiction of regional life and its subtle undercurrent of veiled eroticism, turned the eyes of Mexico's young writers back to the provinces. Technically innovative, and with an emphasis on the free association of ideas and unusual adjectival applications, his poetry was a source of inspiration for poets of the vanguard period. Torres Bodet contrasted the influence of González Martínez and López

Velarde in the following terms: "These two influences, so opposite, were fused together in the work of all, or almost all the young poets. From the former, they inherited love of pure form, correct language, a severe intellectual modesty; from the latter, a curiosity for new sensations, the desire for a more original and plastic metaphor, a sense of color and a voluptuous sense of touch."[8]

In an interview with Pellicer by the author on June 5, 1972, the poet said the following about the literary figures who had most influenced him:

The most important poets during my youth, also taking into account my adolescence, were the great poets of modernism. . . . I was influenced by Rubén Darío, by Leopoldo Lugones, and also by José Santos Chocano. During my study for the bachelor's degree, I had Enrique González Martínez as a literature teacher. The impact of González Martínez on my work, however, is very limited. He is a poet of a reflective intimacy which I do not have. I was born in the tropics, as you know. The tropical person is a passionate, sensual person who is not often given to reflection. I met López Velarde when I was twenty, but we were friends for only a year because he died shortly thereafter. There is very little influence of Velarde in my work. In my second book, entitled *Seis, siete poemas* [*Six, Seven Poems*], there are some testimonies to his influence. These poets formed in some manner my poetic criterion, but very shortly after age twenty, I found my own literary orientation toward Latin America and consequently, my works had little in common with European poetry. Some of my companions in the *Contemporáneos* group at that time, such as Salvador Novo, were influenced by the North American poets of that epoch. Villaurrutia was influenced by the English poets and above all, by the French. Torres Bodet was educated in French literature from childhood. Because of the influence of the great Latin American poets and because of my own inclination toward everything ours, everything which was American interested me much more than what was happening in Europe. . . . But these poets were born in the central region and I am from the tropics. In the tropics and in the land where I was born, Tabasco, the Mayan culture flourished. Therefore, the ancient cultures of Mexico have had a level of meaning for me which I would call a passion. My house is full of pre-Columbian art objects and Mexican paintings from Mexico's first great painter, José María Velasco. All this has inclined me more toward nature and hero figures than to anything else. . . .

It was thus against a turbulent background of radical intellectual and political change that Pellicer and a number of other young poets, to be known as the *Contemporáneos,* began their literary careers. Inspired in the equally revolutionary orientation of the *Ateneo,* these writers were later to produce a body of impressive literature which would rank their generation as among the most important in twentieth-century Mexican letters. I shall elaborate further on Pellicer's relation to this group in the third section of this chapter. But first a few facts about Pellicer's youth.

II *Early Years and Education*

Carlos Pellicer Cámara was born in the colonial city of Villahermosa, Tabasco, on November 4, 1899. The son of Carlos Pellicer, an army colonel who had fought in the revolutionary forces of Alvaro Obregón (1880–1928), and Deifilia Cámara de Pellicer, he was deeply influenced by the tropical setting of his native region. In an interview with the Mexican critic Emmanuel Carballo in 1965, Pellicer stressed the importance of his early years on his writings:

My friends were educated in the Valley of Mexico. Even though I have spent most of my life in the Valley of Mexico, one must not forget that one's childhood is a very influential period. The things that happened to me in Tabasco, the death of my brother Ernesto, my first trip to the sea, my love for my mother, are impressions and emotions that matured, slowly, and influenced what I later did or put into action with language. All these things continue to influence my life. I have been totally a man from the tropics.[9]

Due to the vicissitudes of the Revolution, Pellicer's father, now retired from the army, moved his family to the capital city around 1912 and established a small pharmacy. Carlos was able to cultivate the friendship of a number of literary luminaries of the day in the halls of the famed *Escuela Nacional Preparatoria* (National Preparatory School). They were Rubén M. Campos (1876–1945), who first introduced him to the study of pre-Hispanic art, Luis G. Urbina (1864–1934), the dean of Mexican literary criticism of that era, and the modernist poet, Amado Nervo. It was during these years, too, that Pellicer heard the Peruvian modernist poet José Santos Chocano (1875–1934) recite some of his verse in the auditorium of the *Escuela Preparatoria.* The lush tropical imagery and Pan-American spirit of Chocano's verse impressed him so deeply that Pellicer was to later count him among his principal sources of inspiration.

III *The* Contemporáneos *Group*

Pellicer's association with a number of y ng literati at the *Pre-paratoria* and later at the *Escuela de Altos Estudios* (School of Superior Studies) was to prove germinal in s career as a poet. These young men, who later came to be known as the *Contem-poráneos*, were mutually influenced by the members of the *Ateneo de México* and collaborated themselves on a series of literary re-views from about 1916 to 1931. In recalling this loosely knit associa-tion of friends, Torres Bodet referred to Pellicer in the following terms: "a pale, well-dressed young man, with penetrating eyes, thick eyelashes . . . masculine. . . . Like his poems the first thing his person manifested was adjectives: his thick silk tie, his bright socks; and on his ring finger a splendid solitaire."[10]

As early as 1916, this group of friends began a more formal associ-ation with the publication of the ephemeral review, *Gladios*, founded and coedited by Octavio Barreda and Pellicer. The review contained some of Pellicer's earliest published verse, "Sonetos romanos" ("Roman Sonnets"). This venture was followed in 1918 by the weekly magazine, *San-Ev-Ank*, which had some twenty num-bers. Pellicer characterized it as "an iconoclastic combative sheet that caused more than one quarrel with members of the faculty."[11] In 1918, this group of friends reaffirmed its solidarity by forming a new atheneum, *El Ateneo de la Juventud (The Atheneum of Youth)*. Torres Bodet described the group as distinct from the *Ateneo de México* in its makeup and to a large measure its goals: "This group, in which . . . the names of Carlos Pellicer, Martín Gómez Palacio, Bernardo Ortiz de Montellano, José Gorostiza, and Enrique Gon-zález Rojo appeared, was conceived with such elasticity that it could subsist without opposing the liberty of the individual members."[12] The publication of *México Moderno* (1920–1923), edited by the poet Enrique González Martínez, was an even more impressive under-taking. The sixteen issues of the journal, published between August, 1920, and June, 1923, contained contributions from all the principal members of the literary generation. Torres Bodet directed a section dedicated to the review of European belles lettres, "Letras europeas" ("European Letters"), and Salvador Novo was in charge of "Repertorio" ("Repertory"), selections of translations from foreign reviews. Poetry and creative writing by José Gorostiza and Ortiz de

Montellano were presented, as well as essays by Ermilo Abreu Gómez, Samuel Ramos, and Francisco Monterde.

A more obvious organ of group thought was *La Falange*. Directed by Torres Bodet and Ortiz de Montellano, it was published in seven issues from December, 1922, to October, 1923. Similar to *México Moderno*, it contained contributions of creative writing and literary criticism by the *Contemporáneos*. Torres Bodet directed *Glosario*, a section dedicated to the review of current Mexican publications, while Ortiz de Montellano and Xavier Villaurrutia contributed translations of French authors.

Although it was not directed by a member of the *Contemporáneos*, the journal *Antena* also played a significant role in the history of the literary generation. Issued in five numbers from July to November, 1924, under the joint editorship of Francisco Monterde and García Icazbalceta, it contained selections by Ortiz de Montellano, José Gorostiza, Torres Bodet, Enrique González Rojo, Salvador Novo, Jorge Cuesta, and Xavier Villaurrutia. Of particular importance was the staunch apolitical position maintained by the editors. Accordingly, in the second issue the following editorial note appeared: "This review is not the mouthpiece of a literary or political group. . . . We are prepared to recognize all intellectual values without blindly accepting or rejecting established ones or unknown ones."[13]

Ulises was typical of the increasingly apolitical, aesthetic orientation of the reviews in which the *Contemporáneos* participated. Edited by Novo and Villaurrutia, it was published in six issues between May, 1927, and February 1928. Like *La Falange* and *Antena*, the editors claimed no involvement in political affairs. They wrote, "It is honorable to declare that *Ulises* does not represent in any way the 'national feeling.'"[14]

From the experiences of these young writers with literary magazines came the journal *Contemporáneos* (1928–1931), the review after which the group was named.[15] Founded by Bernardo J. Gastélum (1899–), Torres Bodet, Ortiz de Montellano, and González Rojo, the review was fashioned after the prestigious Spanish *Revista de Occidente* and the French, *Nouvelle Revue Française*. This journal contained many of the features of the earlier literary periodicals such as the inclusion of art reproductions, a marked interest in European literature, and an essentially apolitical editorial policy. It also presented extensive contributions by writers like Abreu Gómez, Samuel Ramos, Genaro Estrada, José Romano Muñoz, and Carlos Díaz Dufóo who were usually considered outside of the literary generation *(Contemporáneos)*, but who had made important contributions to the group's earlier ventures in *La Falange, Antena,* and *Ulises.*

The publication of the review marked the high watermark in the association of the group. After its cessation, many of the poets secured diplomatic or governmental positions and began to forge more independent literary reputations. It is important to note that while Pellicer was a more active participant in the earlier group endeavors *(Gladios, San-Ev-Ank, México Moderno, Antena),* he was only tangentially involved in the publication of *Contemporáneos.* For while his school friends were immersing themselves in the currents of European vanguardism, Pellicer was forging a distinct image as a spokesman for Pan-American union and as a champion of liberal thought.

To more fully understand the unique position Pellicer has held in the history of contemporary Mexican literature, it is necessary to more closely examine his relationship with this group of writers known as the *Contemporáneos.* Pellicer's ambivalent relationship to his contemporaries can only be appreciated against the background of this important review. More important than the close personal relationships these writers established, beginning with their friendships in the *Escuela Nacional Preparatoria* were the common attitudes they shared about art and politics.

Repeatedly in the pages of *Contemporáneos,* these young men explained and defended their essentially apolitical stance with reference to artistic experience. In opposition to the strongly propagandistic orientation of other magazines of the period, such as *Crisol,* the editors of *Contemporáneos* rarely commented on the more immediate political and economic consequences of the Revolution. They chose instead to discuss the question of Mexican identity in terms of the aesthetic and philosophical problems which sprang from the Revolution of 1910. The most important commentary of this nature is found in a series of short articles and essays in which the editors defined the role of *Contemporáneos* in Mexican letters. A recurrent theme in all of these is the intrinsic value of Mexico's novel of the Revolution.

Bernardo Ortiz de Montellano, the editor of the journal from issue one to forty-three, treated the theme in three important essays: "Conversation Notes,"[16] "Literature of the Revolution and Revolutionary Literature,"[17] and "Outline of Modern Mexican Literature."[18] In "Conversation Notes," a penetrating discussion of the function of literature, he compared the body of literature produced in Russia after the Revolution of 1917 with its Mexican counterpart. He notes that, unlike the works written in the Soviet Union, Mexican literature of the Revolution does not reflect any particular social dogma. He argues that the works of Mariano Azuela and Martín Luis Guzmán are masterpieces, because they are not propagandistic: "Good art is individualized and, by obligation and with foresight, should not be mixed with collective social movements."[19] Literature is revolutionary in itself, he continued, and should be judged by its own norms: "Art is not revolutionary because it speaks about or displays the material phenomena of the Revolution; it is revolutionary in itself and by itself. (During the Renaissance, did the theme of Christianity define the artistic quality of the painters?)"[20]

The same thesis was reiterated in "Literature of the Revolution." Although principally a review of a translation of *The Underdogs (Los de abajo)* the essay ends with an observation on the importance of the Mexican Revolution in the arts. Ortiz de Montellano maintains that it is not the theme of the Revolution which will create a body of enduring national literature but rather the seeds of change which it planted: "What the Mexican Revolution succeeded in doing with the new generation of writers, who had been obliged to experience the bitter reality of the Revolution since childhood, was to convince them of the existence of a personal sensibility, more personal and at the same time more genuinely Mexican, which they had to penetrate without losing contact with world culture."[21]

In his well-known survey of Mexican literature, "Outline of Modern Mexican Literature," the Mexican Revolution is again discussed in terms of its catalytic effect on Mexican letters. After tracing the origins of contemporary thought to the intellectual activity and alert universal curiosity of the members of the *Ateneo de la Juventud* ("Literary Society of the Young"), the author declares that the stimulus of the latter *Atenistas* ("Members of the Group") has channeled Mexican letters toward a more universal interpretation of national problems. For Ortiz de Montellano the most transcendental consequence of the Mexican Revolution is not to be seen in the novel of the Revolution, but in the new aesthetic postures adopted by its authors: "As we pointed out with reference to the poetry of López Velarde, the benefits, the influence of the Mexican Revolution on art ought to be sought, rather than in the immediate fruits which come from the tree of our novelists' deeds, in that seed which can bring to their works a new sense of spiritual values, with vistas toward the true tone of Mexican sensibility, culture, and universal ideas."[22]

Reiterating the basic credo of the *Contemporáneos*, Ortiz de Montellano describes the new literary generation as a group destined to interpret its nation's problems within a framework of universality: "All the writers who consciously live the life of their country—its problems, its tradition, its sensibility—have to reflect it in universal forms, the first condition of culture and aspiration of modern man."[23] In addition to these direct references to the Revolution, Ortiz de Montellano alluded to the problem in more general terms in several short notes. The director emphasized repeatedly his belief that literature should not be a vehicle for propaganda. Thus in his note, "New Mexican Journals," he warned the editors of *Crisol* not to let their journal become a mouthpiece for political dogma: "Therefore we praise the attitude of the editors of *Crisol* . . . because we feel that the Mexican Revolution needs a truly profound study of its goals rather than a vain or individualistic literature. *Crisol* has the obligation, in accordance with its goals, to determine, with profundity and wisdom, the ideals of the Revolution, only being careful not to fall into contemporary politics."[24]

Jaime Torres Bodet voiced much the same point of view in two important essays on contemporary Mexican literature, "Approach to López Velarde" and "Perspective of Contemporary Mexican Literature." "Perspective of Contemporary Mexican Literature" is one of the most important sources for the study of the *Contemporáneos*. In his essay, Torres Bodet discusses the intellectual forces which have shaped contemporary Mexican letters and enumerates the principal young creative writers. His introductory comments, a defense of the journal's apolitical, aesthetic position, form one of the group's most precise manifestoes: "Our literature has been accused of a deliberate separation (deliberate?) of its themes from those themes which are offered by national realities. Some writers think they have seen in this attitude of Mexico's new artists, a return to the doctrine of art-for-art's sake. Not content with merely pointing this out, these young artists thought that the act of stating this discovery was tantamount to accusing them of being misguided, without realizing that the most deplorable disorientation was their own, and that beauty rarely serves as a political arm without losing some of its austere perfection."[25]

While Ortiz de Montellano and Jaime Torres Bodet discussed the Mexican Revolution in purely literary terms, Dr. Bernardo Gastélum analyzed the philosophical implications of the civil crisis. Much like his contemporaries, Samuel Ramos and E. Martínez Ulloa, Gastélum was concerned with the revitalization of Mexican intellectual thought. Reflecting the essentially dynamic, activist orientation of the philosophy of José Ortega y Gasset (1883–1953), Gastélum called for a reevaluation of contemporary beliefs. In his essay "Spirit of the Hero," which served as somewhat of a manifesto for the *Contemporáneos,* he pleaded, "Let us build with these values—in the present—the style of a new ethical sensibility and abandon the absurdity of searching in the ruins of a past that was."[26]

The examination of Mexico's role in music and the plastic arts also was a popular essay theme. Among the most important studies of this nature were: Samuel Ramos, "The Dream of Diego"; Gabriel García Maroto, "The Work of Diego Rivera"; Jean Charlot, "Carlos Mérida and Painting"; and León Pacheco, "The Painting of Rodríguez Lozano." García Marotos' controversial essay on Rivera is typical of the journal's preoccupation with cultural universality. Throughout the essay García Maroto describes with great exactness the techniques Rivera employed to treat Mexican social themes. His attitude toward the function of art is similar to the views advanced by Ortiz de Montellano and Jaime Torres Bodet: "The frescos of Diego Rivera, through the people depicted, tell, sing, curse, and surprise the soul—they try to surprise it at least—with violence and harshness. They endeavor to transport the spectator to a land alien to perfect aesthetic value; they make art a sociopolitical instrument, a mechanized instrument, mechanistic and little refined, and in this dangerous digression which shapes the artist's way, certain initial virtues become blurry, giving way to despair, oratory, and ironic gesticulation."[27]

The most significant allusions to the Mexican Revolution, however, are to be found in the journal's expositional prose. With the limited exception of works by Mariano Azuela, Celestino Gorostiza, Rubén Salazar Mallén, and Julio Jiménez Rueda, the theme was rarely reflected in the journal's repertoire of creative writing. When it did appear, as in the writings of the aforementioned writers, it served primarily as a backdrop for the development of psychological themes. The comments which appeared in *Contemporáneos* concerning Azuela's *La malhora* shed some light on the question of the magazine's motivation. Valéry Larbaud, in his prologue to *Los de abajo (The Underdogs)*, did not hesitate to affirm its importance. Ortiz de Montellano concurred: "For my part, I don't hesitate in saying that I prefer *La malhora* . . . the next to the last of Azuela's publications."[28]

While the editor's preference for *La malhora* over *The Underdogs* may be a completely unjustifiable critical stand, it highlights the magazine's attitude toward social literature in general and literature of the Mexican Revolution in particular. Thus, while the editors presented a number of important essays treating Revolutionary themes, they vehemently defended the position of the writer as creator or interpreter of phenomena rather than as a mouthpiece for political propaganda. The unique posture of the *Contemporáneos* with reference to the problem of the Mexican identity marks an important phase in the development of Mexican thought. The members of the group may be classified as vanguardists in art, for they sought to bring Mexican literature into contact with the currents of European postwar thought (futurism, dadaism, surrealism) and to break sharply with their own literary past. As a consequence, the writings of the group and above all, their poetry, were characterized by a general movement toward thematic and stylistic complexity. With reference to thematic elements, the poetry of the *Contemporáneos* was highly introspective. Xavier Villaurrutia examined man's ubiquitous fear of death and solitude in his *Nocturnos (Nocturnes)*, while Ortiz de Montellano examined the oneiric world of the subconscious in *Sueños (Dreams)*, and Jaime Torres Bodet depicted the anguish of a dehumanized, technological world in *Destierro (Exile)*.

Pellicer's optimistic work stands in sharp contrast to the philosophical orientation and fixation with death of the *Contemporáneos*. The very titles of his books—*Colors in the Sea, Hour of June*—suggest a joy in living which is opposite to his contemporaries' themes.

Some of the earliest commentary on the poet, written by members of the group itself, evinces a tendency to emphasize the differences between Pellicer and the other *Contemporáneos*. The comments of Xavier Villaurrutia, which appeared in the short-lived review *Ulises*, typify this posture: "For Pellicer, poetry has been a trip around the world instead of a trip into the subconscious, which up to now poetry has been for us. . . ."[29] Jorge Cuesta commented on the orientation of Pellicer's verse in the controversial *Antología de la poesía mexicana moderna (Anthology of Modern Mexican Poetry)*: "The Contemporáneos continue to be attentive to the poetic development of this 'extemporáneo' Pellicer, the traveling poet; some apparently admire his poetry. However, they can also attack him for everything that makes Pellicer a different poet. But it is useless to search in his verse for any tendency which is not exclusively that of complete enjoyment of the senses."[30] Bernardo Ortiz de Montellano echoed the same thought in a review of *Camino (Highway)* which appeared in *Contemporáneos*: "A conserver of the musical instruments of poetry, distant from Góngora, Mallarmé, Valéry, he recreates the joy of words, just as they ought to sound in the ear, in a sense parallel to what, in modern music, is achieved by the new rhythms of jazz."[31] In his autobiography, *Tiempo de arena (Time of Sand)*, Jaime Torres Bodet synthesized the attitude of the *Contemporáneos* when he spoke of Pellicer's poetry: "Music and color were the qualities of these poems. The metaphors became separated at times from the depths of the composition; at times the unity of theme became secondary. . . . But how many plastic suggestions those Alexandrians contained!"[32]

The propensity to concentrate exclusively on the chromatic and musical effects of Pellicer's verse has been perpetuated by the early translators of Pellicer in the United States. The comments of Edna Worthley Underwood reflect this attitude: "He seems to be a painter who happened to be forced to use the pen and black ink instead of brush and bright colors. No one can read anything of his without being impressed first of all with his color sense, and secondly with that sense of form that we always associate with the plastic arts."[33] In a later translation, the editors restated the same thesis: "Pellicer is an impressionist, creating such vivid harmonies of color and form that the poetic pattern is frequently subjugated and at times seems wholly lost."[34] Ironically, while the members of the generation *Contemporáneos* subtly disassociated Pellicer from the group, Hispanists have constantly linked him with these poets. As a consequence, most discussions of Pellicer's verse focus on the differences between him and his more experimental cohorts.

More recent criticism has justly tended to exclude Pellicer from the generation *Contemporáneos*. Although he must certainly be studied in relation to the group, in a conceptual sense he was not a member of the generation. Pellicer's concern for Mexico's indigenous past, his decrying of the injustices of political domination, and his aloofness from experimental verse forms, clearly puts him at odds with the other *Contemporáneos*. Once he has been distinguished from this group, his importance as a unique force in contemporary Mexican letters begins to emerge. The tendency to consider Pellicer as a mere painter with words, a second-class poet of the *Contemporáneos*, has begun to subside. As early as 1944, Manuel Lerín asserted, "The poetry of Pellicer is not so superficial— lacking in depth—as has been said."[35] Carlos González Salas, in the distinguished *Cuadernos Hispanoamericanos*, also made note of the more transcendental aspects of his poetry.[36] Likewise, in his study on Pellicer, Frank Dauster declared, "Therefore, it seems unjust that he continues to be tagged as a landscape poet; for him poetry means union of man with nature."[37]

With the publication of his collected poems, *Material poético* (1962), Pellicer received an even more objective and thoroughgoing examination. In a review of this book in the *Times Literary Supplement*, he is linked with Octavio Paz as a poet of first importance by international standards.[38] The recent publication of *Carlos Pellicer: Primera antología poética* by the Fondo de Cultura Económica, the extensive "Aportación bibliográfica" by Pedro F. de Andrea and George Melynkovich, and the increased space alloted him in several important anthologies of Hispanic verse in the United States signal a growing awareness of the importance of Pellicer.[39]

IV *The Traveling Poet*

With the possible exception of Torres Bodet, Pellicer was the most widely traveled of the young poets. Upon the completion of his studies at the *Preparatoria*, Pellicer was elected the first representative of the newly formed Federation of Mexican Students and traveled to Bogotá, Colombia. He met Germán Arciniegas there and collaborated on the organization of a Federation of Colombian students, an act which displeased the Colombian government and forced him to move on to Venezuela. When his attempts at organizing students in Venezuela also met with disfavor, Pellicer returned to Mexico in 1920. He participated there in a demonstration against the Venezuelan government and published the following epithet in the review *Maestro:* "Friends: on the border of the universe where due to the kindness of the Gods Simón Bolívar, the most wonderful of men and the Liberator of America was born, treason and murder defile that part of the world called Venezuela."[40] That same year he met José Vasconcelos, who had heard of his activities and retained him as an assistant. In 1921, Pellicer accompanied Vasconcelos, then minister of education under the Obregón regime (1920–1925), on a cultural mission to Latin America. The same year was published Pellicer's first collection of verse, *Colores en el mar y otros poemas (Colors in the Sea and Other Poems).* It reflected many of Vasconcelos' Americanist ideas and signaled an emerging interest in indigenous culture. This was followed in 1924 by the publication of two more books of verse, *Piedra de sacrificios (Sacrificial Stone)* and *Seis, siete poemas (Six, Seven Poems).* The former, which bore a prologue by Vasconcelos, is of particular interest because of the militant tone and bitter anti-United States feeling of some of its verses.

In 1925, the year his brief biography of the liberator Simón Bolívar was published, Pellicer again left Mexico. A study tour of Europe was made possible through the generosity of the Argentine writer José Ingenieros (1877–1925). After a year of residence in Paris, he traveled to Egypt, Italy, and later in the company of Vasconcelos, throughout the Middle East. In 1927, Pellicer returned to Paris. It was there that his next book, *Hora y veinte (One Twenty)* was published. During his second stay in the French capital, he was introduced to the Mexican painter, Francisco Iturbe. A great patron of the arts, Iturbe hired Pellicer as his secretary and took him on yet another tour of the Near East. The impressions of this journey were included in *Camino (Highway)* published in 1929.

Upon his return to Mexico in 1929, Pellicer again became involved in politics. During Vasconcelos' campaign for president, a student was assassinated. Pellicer read the funeral eulogy and was later associated with a plot to assassinate presidential candidate Pascual Ortiz Rubio. As a consequence of his identification with the opposition party, Pellicer was jailed for some two months in 1920. During his stay in prison he became acquainted with the Marxist novelist José Revueltas (1914–).

Much like other Spanish American poets before him (Rubén Darío, José Martí, and Jorge Luis Borges), Pellicer traveled at least on two occasions to Spain. During his first visit in 1931, he briefly met Federico García Lorca. Pellicer later described the encounter in these terms: "He brought with him all the light of his native Andalusia . . . the fleeting vision of that Gypsy singer remains in my memory. I later learned from Salvador Novo that Federico had spoken enthusiastically to him of some of my poems in the book, *Palomas* [*Doves*]."[41] During this first visit, Pellicer also met the Spanish critic Enrique Díez Canedo (1879–1944), the essayist Eugenio d'Ors (1882–1954), and the novelist and poet Ramón del Valle-Inclán (1866–1936). Pellicer returned to Spain in 1937 for a congress of writers in Valencia. It was during this visit that he met Rafael Alberti, Juan Ramón Jiménez, and Miguel Hernández, who were members of the so-called "Generation of 1927."

Although Pellicer published a number of shorter poems in the early 1930s—*Cinco poemas* (*Five Poems*, 1931); *Esquemas para una oda tropical* (*Sketches for a tropical ode*, 1933); *Estrophas del mar marino* (*Strophes of the Maritime Sea*, 1934)—his next extensive collection of verse *Hora de junio* (*Hour of June*) appeared in 1937. It was followed in 1941 by the publication of two more books, *Recinto* (*Enclosure*) and *Exágonos* (*Hexagons*). *Subordinaciones* (*Subordinations*), dedicated to the Nobel laureate Gabriela Mistral, followed in 1949. After a lapse of some seven years, the poet brought out *Práctica de vuelo* (*Practice of Flight*), a collection of eighty-seven religious sonnets, in 1956. In 1962, all of Pellicer's previously published poems, together with some uncollected ones, were published in a deluxe edition, the *Material poético* (*Poetic Material 1918–1961*) by the press of the National University of Mexico. This same year, Pellicer augmented his earlier poem *Piedra de sacrificios* (*Sacrificial Stone*) and published it under the title *Con palabras y fuego* (*With Words and Fire*). His most recent lengthy poem has been *Teotihuacán y el trece de Agosto* (*Teotihuacán and August the 13th: the Destruction of Tenochtitlán*), dedicated to President Adolfo López Mateos and published in 1965.

Although Pellicer's reputation as a writer rests largely on his poetry, in recent years he has begun to distinguish himself as a museologist. He has been director of the Palacio de Bellas Artes and has written a guide to the Museum of Tabasco, *Museo de Tabasco, Guía Oficial* (1959) and an essay on mural painting in *La pintura mural de la Revolución Mexicana 1921–1960 (Mural Painting and the Mexican Revolution 1921–1960,* 1960), in addition to other essays on the plastic arts. In 1953, Pellicer became a member of the Mexican Academy of the Language and in 1956, was elected president of the Latin American Congress of Writers.

CHAPTER 2

The Early Poetry:
The Animated Tropics

I Colors in the Sea

EARLY in his career, the Mexican poet Xavier Villaurrutia came forth with a comment on poetry which was to be constantly linked with the *Contemporáneos* group. He wrote, "For me, poetry which is a pure external game or delight of the senses has no meaning. The musicality of a verse, the beauty of certain words, does not interest me at all when it is sought as the intent of poetry."[1] Ironically, the exact opposite of this formulation is what best characterizes the verse of Pellicer. Yet writing for Pellicer was not conceived of as an intellectual process; rather, it was a moment of unpremeditated spontaneity. In an interview with Emmanuel Carballo, he described the poetic process in the following terms: "The impulse is so strong that my words, even when they are not ordered with precision, act as if I were within them. For this very reason they are without order, because I *am* their disorder."[2]

Pellicer has reiterated his anti-intellectual concept of the creative act in a number of poems. In *"Nocturno"* ("Nocturne") published in *6, 7 poemas*, he equated the act of writing verse to an uncontrolled flow of emotion: "I don't have time to examine things/ I almost guess them./ An innate and jealous wisdom/ gives me foreseen visions and sudden trills." ("No tengo tiempo de mirar las cosas/ casi las adivino/ Una sabiduría ingénita y celosa/ me da miradas previas y repetinos trinos" [131]).[3] Later in *Hora de junio (Hour of June)*, the act of composition was compared to a form of divine creation; while in such collections as *Recinto (Corner)* and *Camino (Highway)*, it is personified to express its elusive nature.

Pellicer's earliest poems, "Grecia" ("Greece") and "Sonetos Romanos" ("Roman Sonnets"), were published in the review *Gladios* in 1916 and clearly evince a debt to the modernists in their

32

emphasis on chiseled exotic detail. The poet's first book-length collection of verse, *Colores en el mar y otros poemas* (*Colors in the Sea and other poems*, 1921), however, represents a departure from his early dependence on modernist models. Illustrated by his friend Roberto Montenegro, it bore a dedication to the recently deceased poet Ramón López Velarde. The book is largely a collection of landscapes, seascapes, and travel poems, the fruition of his journey to Colombia and Venezuela as a member of Mexican Federation of Students and his later travels to Brazil with José Vasconcelos. In this brief edition of thirty-three poems, Pellicer initiated a number of basic thematic concerns which were to recur throughout his later poetry. The first poem, a simple statement of faith, synthesizes a number of the poet's basic philosophies and sets the tone for the book:

> In the midst of my life's fortune
> I stop to say that the world is good
> because of the blood Christ shed. . . .
>
> My heart, Savior, like a poem
> climbs life's stairway
> and gives you its love like a gem. . . .
>
> En medio de la dicha de mi vida
> deténgome a decir que el mundo es bueno
> por la divina sangre de la herida. . . .
>
> Mi corazón, Señor, como el poema,
> sube la escalinata de la vida
> y te da su pasión como una gema. . . .
>
> (9)

After establishing his pervasive joy in living and his equally firm commitment to Christian doctrine, Pellicer wrote a brief note on the importance of the sea in his verse: "The sea—which is not a physical aspect of the world, but rather a spiritual attitude—has captured my heart and made me its subject. Because of a dynamic longing which controls my spirit, the vast area where the waters move has attracted me exceedingly. Shores of Mexico, Colombia, Venezuela—unforgettable republics where for two years I represented Mexican students—beaches of Cuba, sonorous beaches of the Atlantic, proud beaches of the Pacific, the salt and wind of your panoramas have invaded my blood, coloring it with your memories."[4] This statement precedes the first of three thematic groups of poems: (1) twenty-five short seascapes and landscapes; (2) two longer descriptions of an exotic dancer; and (3) finally, a loosely knit group of poems centered on various sites in the Andes together with a sonnet to Simón Bolívar.

There is a certain aptness in considering *Colores en el mar* germinal to Pellicer's entire career as a poet, for although his work grew in terms of thematic variety and technical complexity, he never substantially veered from the basic poetic orientation established here. One is at once struck by the poet's debt to the plastic arts. The first twenty-five selections, which present definite pictures and colors, call to mind the works of Claude Monet, George Braque, and Rufino Tamayo. Pellicer himself has on many occasions emphatically stated his closeness to painting: "My affinity with painters is immediate. I have always felt that music is the most important expression of poetry. Painting and words follow next in descending order. If I admit that color and brush stroke are nearer to what I write than words, it is easy to understand why I have always lived closer to painters than writers."[5]

Almost all these initial poems are efforts to represent the multifaceted pictorial possibilities of the tropical sea. The sun emerges as the dominant image in the first poem, which is a collage of six separate but complementary images related to the power of the tropic sun—a symbol which for Pellicer often achieves almost archetypal proportions:

> "The sun! The sun! The sun! . . .
> Behind a red cloud
> that young sun arrived. . . .
>
> Clouds in *sol* major
> and waves in *la* minor.
>
> Life was as beautiful as the dawn.
>
> It seemed like a thousand children were swimming in the sea
> the waves were like that
> all childlike and sonorous

And a woman went by
dressed in her Sunday best.

¡El Sol! ¡El Sol! ¡El Sol! . . .
Detrás de un arrebol
llegó aquel joven Sol. . . .

Nubes en *sol* mayor
y olas en *la* menor.

La vida era tan bella como el amanecer.

Pareció que en el mar
se bañasen mil niños; así las olas eran
infantiles y claras de gritar.

Y una mujer pasaba
toda dominical.

(13)

II "*The Sun*"

"El sol" ("The Sun") is a telling poem inasmuch as it typifies not merely the technical aspects of Pellicer's early poetry but sheds some light on his attitude toward reality as well. At first glance, it may seem to be a traditional, descriptive poem. A closer examination reveals that it is not a transcription in normative poetic terms of some external visual phenomenon but rather an attempt to recreate a mental image of something experienced by means of juxtaposing separate but connected impressions, all of which attempt the re-creation of the single impression of dawn rising on a seaside morning. Pellicer moves from a simple personification in the first stanza, where the sun is presented as a young man, to a comparison of waves and clouds in terms of notes on the musical scale in the second, to a strikingly elemental simile in the fourth. The last verses suddenly shift back to the terrestrial and the mundane by evoking a somewhat conventionalized image of a well-dressed woman. In effect, the poet seems to be manipulating several different types of poetic conceits on simultaneous planes; hence reality appears not to be described but created.

Another feature of these early poems is the attention given to

certain dominant colors, above all, aqua, blue, and green. In particular, three poems attempt a color transcription in which Pellicer
establishes a link between color and emotion:

Blue

The sky painted blue.
The sea painted blue.
Man's spirit set free in blue.

The day played its golden ace
and lost it in so much blue.

And silence said in chorus:
Tomorrow there will be no blue.

Azul

Pintado el cielo en azul.
El mar pintado en azul.
El alma suelta en azul.

Azul.

Azul.

El día jugó su as de oro
y lo perdió en tanto azul.

Y el silencio dijo en coro:
"Ya mañana no hay azul!"

(16)

And again:

Blue afternoon, blue waters, tranquil desolation.
Clouds abandoned on another shore. . . .

A flight of grey birds form a single slow line. . . .

Tarde azul, agua azul, desolación tranquila.
Nubes abandonadas sobre otro litoral.

Vuelo de grises pájaros su lento viaje ahila.

(22)

This first short piece betrays a structural pattern which was to be repeated often in Pellicer's poetry: an initial descriptive allusion (here a reference to the blueness of the sky) followed by a startling shift in perspective, as in this case where the day becomes a card player. Pellicer demonstrated in early poems such as this a marked ability to play with the reader's sense of anticipation, since he often began his poems with a diction well within the bounds of the established formulaic poetic language of his day, only to insert an image clearly at odds with such preconceived conventions.

There is also a noticeable tendency to focus on the iridescent colors typical of seaside landscapes. Most frequently, the poet uses verbs to describe these hues: "The afternoon gilded its blood/ and the wind gilded its voice" ("La tarde doraba su sangre/ y el viento doraba su voz" [19]). And another: "The sea made its figures transparent/ during that carnival-like day" ("El día diafanizaba sus figuras/ en aquel medio día carnavalesco" [20]). On a more limited scale, he employs adjectives alone: "During that opaline afternoon, in front of the sea of Campeche/ the nuptial Atlantic shadows watch me" ("En la tarde opalina, frente al mar de Campeche/ las penumbras atlánticas me velan" [17]). Simply stated, what seems to give these poems their so-called "plasticity" derives in part from a recurrent interplay of hues. Because of his propensity to deal with color as an integral, verbal part of the poem, Pellicer's verses often do not appear excessively gilded, ornamental, or adjectival. "Apuntes coloridos" is perhaps Pellicer's *tour de force* with chromatic imagery. A description of the multifaceted hues of a tropical setting, it is distinguished by an emphasis on tactile imagery. Color becomes concretized:

> In the sky there is a dance of clouds.
> The lake copies the best lines
> and the stolen white shadows
> are gilded and painted in the afternoon.
> The lake becomes a magic painting in colors
> where I touch forms and drink color.
> . . . .
> If I were to dip my hands in the lake,
> they would be blue forever.
> The landscape is so clear
> and there is a sweet moving peace.

En el cielo hay una danza de nubes.
El lago copia las mejores líneas
y las robadas sombras blancas
en la tarde se doran y se pintan.
Se torna el lago mágica acuarela
en las que formas toco y bebo tintas.

Si mojara mis manos en el lago
me quedarían azules para siempre.
El paisaje es más claro
y hay una dulce paz, conmovedoramente.

(54)

In a great number of these pieces, Pellicer creates the impression
that he is describing the scene to the reader, somewhat like a critic
might point out the color lines and geometrical shapes of a painting,
and thus achieves a degree of poetic objectivity. These selections
show the same basic architectural plan as others—a series of rela-
tively independent strophe-images linked by similarity of tone or
mood. In the three strophe, "Noche sin sombra" ("Night Without
Shadows"), for example, a solitary ship at sea is first equated to a
bird in flight over the vast sea. This is followed by a description of
light playing off the waves which culminates with a more objective
portrait of a vessel:

Night of terror and glory
Alone, amid the crystaline mystery of the sea,
Seeing the moon live and telling a story
desolate and somber of a solitary ship.

Noche de terror y de gloria. . . .
Solos, en el misterio cristalino del mar,
viendo vivir la Luna y contando una historia
desolada y sombría de un buzo singular.

(24)

Perhaps one of the best of Pellicer's portrait poems is "Mira como
se van esas nubes de otoño" ("Look at how those autumn clouds go
by"). Pellicer directly addresses the reader here with a surprisingly
elemental poetic diction:

Look how the autumn clouds go away
Spread out the length of the quiet sea.
Look how these autumn clouds go away
like ships from some fable which will
soon return again.

September is that man casting out his nets
melancholically, not feeling like fishing.
. . . You see the first star? Take hold of it, if you can
comprehend the infinite desolation of the sea.

Mira como se van esas nubes de otoño
tendidas a lo largo del largo y quieto mar.
Mira como se van esas nubes de otoño
como naves de fábula que pronto volverán.

Septiembre es ese hombre que está echando sus redes
melancólicamente, sin ganas de pescar.
. . . ¿Ves la primera estrella? Asúmela, si puedes
comprender la infinita desolación del mar.

(27)

As the critic Luis Rius has pointed out, there is a certain childlike
candor and freshness in the imagery of *Colores en el mar,* because it
is derived chiefly through elemental personifications of the natural
world: "The waves were taking a bath" ("las olas se estaban
bañando" [15]); "The sun was already old but he was king" ("El sol
ya estaba viejo, pero era un rey" [18]), and unusual linkages such as
"Like a sea faun I followed that wave/ Loose hair and undulating
blue waist" ("Como fauna marino perseguí aquella ola/ suelta la
cabellera y el talle azul-ondeante" [18]).

III *"Study"*

At times the poet appears to stand back and comment on his own
propensity to play optical games with color, air, and light. "Estudio"
("Study"), dedicated to the critic Pedro Henríquez Ureña, is one of
Pellicer's first autocritical moments as well as one of his most often
quoted poems. Unlike many of the poems in *Colores en el mar,* it is
written in the first person as an uninterrupted block of poetic narrative:

Study

I shall play with the houses of Curaçao.
I shall put the sea on the left
and make more bridges that sway.
So says the poet!
We are in Holland and America too,
and this is a toyshop isle,
where the laws are a queen's
and doors and windows smile.
With the strings of the lyre
and the handkerchiefs of the voyage,
we shall make sails for boats
that never go anywhere.
Government House is far too small
for a Dutch family.
This evening Claude Monet will arrive
to eat blue and electric things.
And up this suspicious alley
we shall send Rembrandt's Night Watch.
. . . give me the port of Curaçao!
        toyshop isle,
        where the laws are a queen's
        and doors and windows smile.[5]

Jugaré con las casas de Curazao,
pondré el mar a la izquierda
y haré mas puentes movedizos.
¡Lo que diga el poeta!
Estamos en Holanda y en América
y es una isla de juguetería,
con decretos de reina
y ventanas y puertas de alegría.
Con las cuerdas de la lira
y los pañuelos del viaje,
haremos velas para los botes
que no van a ninguna parte.
La casa de gobierno es demasiado pequeña
para una familia holandesa.
Por la tarde vendrá Claude Monet
a comer cosas azules y eléctricas.
Y por esa callejuela sospechosa
haremos pasar la Ronda de Rembrandt.

> . . . pásame el puerto de Curazao!
> isla de juguetería,
> con decretos de reina
> y ventanas y puertas de alegría.

(29)

"Estudio" is very important in understanding the aesthetic principles which underlie Pellicer's poetry. This poem, much like "El sol," proves that his early verse was neither particularly traditional nor descriptive. While it is true that many of the images employed are essentially visual, their arrangement, disposition, and structural focus reveal an attempt by the poet not to reproduce reality in the manner of the modernists, but to evoke impressions of an independent and personal "poetic" reality. In this sense, a poem like "Estudio" places Pellicer closer conceptually to the vanguard writers of the 1920s who had proposed a radical departure from descriptive poetry in favor of the creation of a new poetic reality rooted in, but independent of, nature.

The poem's opening lines, while casual and almost conversational in tone, contain an important statement which is essential to the poem's elucidation: the explicit assertion by the writer that he will manipulate the reader's perception of reality. I shall "play," he declares. Immediately in the second line Pellicer establishes a kind of optical-spatial relationship with his audience as he explicitly directs the eye around a poetic bas relief map of Curaçao. The impression that this is a world freed from the normative laws of the physical world is reinforced in lines 6–8 where we are told that this is a "toyshop isle," where "the laws are a queen's" and where even doors and windows "smile." The reference to the Dutch painter Rembrandt and the French artist Monet underscore the poet's intention of evoking through words a set of visual-emotional impressions much like those captured by the master artist. The poet clearly shifts from description to fantasy and wish-fulfilling in the last four lines where he yearns aloud to be carried to the world of his own poetic creation.

Apart from the poem's somewhat innovative narrative structure, the total effect of its reading creates a unique impression. A first scanning of "Estudio" may evoke the feeling that it is a descriptive poem, but a closer study of the component lines shows that the poet has gone beyond the realm of description and the metaphor of analogy: it is a world of anthropomorphic doors and windows, where ships sail to nowhere, and artists consume "blue and electric things." It is a poem of childlike exuberance in which the poet's sense of discovery is conveyed through the deliberate distortion of the ordinary.

The levity of tone in "Estudio" is characteristic of the majority of the poems in *Colores*. There is very little philosophizing in these short pieces. At times, however, Pellicer moves away from pure description to make a comment or simple statement of faith. In these instances, he approaches the verbal economy and tightness of structure of the haiku, an unrhymed Japanese poem of three lines which was influential in imagist verse and had achieved some vogue in Mexico through the influence of José Juan Tablada. Several poems in particular seem to illustrate this technique best: "Sandalia de espuma saqué del océano" ("I picked a sandal of foam from the ocean" [32]), and "Esmaltín en la playa el cangrejo" ("A deep blue crab on the beach" [34]). In the former, a two-stanza piece, there is an observation on the eternal feminine: "Woman who in the seatime night/ betters both land and sea/ Anchor my life" ("Mujer que en la noche marina/ mejoras la tierra y el mar/ Ancla mi vida" [32]).

In sharp contrast to these short poems stand the longer dance pieces, "Dos danzas de Tórtola Valencia" ("Two Dances of Tórtola Valencia"). The first, "La danza del incienso" ("The Incense Dance"), was set to music by Luigini and the second, "La Bayadera" ("The Bayadère"), by Leo Delibes. In both poems, there is an easily perceptible dramatic structure which begins with a description of the entrance of the dancer, follows through with a portrait of the dancer's movements, and culminates in a transcription of the finale:

> And the frenetic movement, jingling in her bracelets
> shining in her clothing, in her sensual torso
> Until the rapture of the endless spiral
> Cast her down amid the scandal of the final crescendo.

> Y era el girar frenético, ruidoso en las ajorcas,
> deslumbrante en las telas, en el torso, sensual.
> ¡Hasta que la embriaguez de la espiral continua
> la rindió entre el escándalo del *crescendo* final!

(43)

The thematic variety of *Colores en el mar* was enhanced by the inclusion of "Recuerdos de los Andes" ("Memories of the Andes"), a group of poems inspired by Pellicer's experiences as a student in Colombia. They evince an early interest in the landscape of Latin America and an overwhelming admiration for Simón Bolívar. The longest of these pieces, "La tempestad en los Andes" ("Storm in the Andes"), was prefaced by the following note: "Three etchings about the storm in the Andes. . . . Through these mountains passed and triumphed Bolívar in 1819, the most generous of men and the greatest of heroes."[6]

The three-part poem marks a change in direction from Pellicer's tightly constructed seascapes. The three poems form one longer, logically connected description of the coming storm, the inundation, and the return of a group of travelers with the coming of light. Much like the dance poems, these pieces build gradually toward a dramatic climax. Importantly, the identification between man and nature, which served more of a decorative function in his other compositions, is here related in a more basic way to the manner in which Pellicer views the fundamental relationship between man and the physical world.

IV *"Memories of Iza"*

"Recuerdos de Iza" ("Memories of Iza"), the poem which follows, however, is clearly more similar to the imagistic tension of "Estudio." Again, the poet demonstrates his skill at assembling multiple, independent images and fusing them into a poetic whole. Here as well, there is also a noticeable movement toward the use of synesthesia, the blending of several responses of the senses into one image:

> 1. One might have thought the town,
>   with the valley behind,
>   had lost its mind
>   and laid the one street down.

> 2. Likewise the mountains, row on row,
>   feverishly, like the spring, got posted below.

> 3. The alcohol upon
>   its windows is blended with the sun.

4. Its women and its flowers
   speak the dialect of colors.

5. And the little stream that gallops away
   runs off with the hens in February and May.

6. Up the sidewalks they go past,
   curate like cow, and the light going last.

7. Here nothing discloses
   a greater transcendence than the roses.[7]

1. Creeríase que la población,
   después de recorrer el valle,
   perdió la razón
   y se trazó una sola calle.

2. Y así bajo la cordillera
   se apostó febrilmente como la primavera.

3. En sus ventanas el alcohol
   está mezclado con sol.

4. Sus mujeres y sus flores
   hablan el dialecto de los colores.

5. Y el riachuelo que corre como un caballo,
   arrastra las gallinas en febrero y en mayo.

6. Pasan por la acera
   lo mismo el cura, que la vaca y que la luz postrera.

7. Aquí no suceden cosas
   de mayor trascendencia que las rosas.

                                                    (53)

"Recuerdos de Iza" is composed of ten stanzas each two lines in
length with the exception of the first which is four verses long. The
typographical arrangement by which each strophe is numbered
suggests that Pellicer was consciously trying to stress the poetic
independence of these two-line strophes. The title "memories"
serves as a thematic matrix for the poem, conferring an organic unity
on what might otherwise be labeled disparate impressions. The

poem almost seems to be a parody of the landscape poetry which flourished after the decline of modernism. In many ways "Recuerdos de Iza" is a deceptive poem inasmuch as it plays with the reader's sense of anticipation. The poet does not evoke a set of predictable visual images, but instead builds a rather gradual montage of synesthetic impressions. Its total effect is powerful: the memory of the village is presented as a multisensory experience rather than a lineal one-dimensional recollection. The poet's desire to capture and express a sense of newness and wonder is effectively conveyed through a "newness" of structure and form.

The closing poem in *Colores en el mar*, a sonnet to Simón Bolívar, evinces yet another facet of Pellicer's personality: an early and pervasive dedication to a number of hero figures. In contrast to the flashy, tactile seascape and landscape poems, "A Bolívar" is carefully wrought in traditional meters. Addressing the patriot in the familiar person, in Spanish a device often used in prayers and supplications, he entreats him to again come to the aid of the Latin American republics:

> Father, here is your nation. Bless it and pardon it. . . .
> . . . .
> Give us your strength, awaken the torch of Dawn
> Which you lighted above the Andes, illuminating the seas.
> Draw your flashing sword across the skies
> And anoint us with the illustrious aloes of your kindness.

> Señor: he aquí a tu pueblo; bendícelo y perdónalo. . . .
> . . . .
> Dónanos tu pujanza, resucita la Aurora
> que encendiste en los Andes iluminando el mar.
> Desnuda sobre el cielo los rayos de tu espada
> y úngenos con los ínclitos áloes de tu bondad.

(56)

The critical reception of *Colores en el mar* was limited. Apart from an enthusiastic descriptive note in the *Verdadera historia de la Revolución Mexicana* (*The True History of the Mexican Revolution*, 1921), edited by Pellicer's friend Alfonso Taracena, there appears to have been no major review of the book. It was not until almost fifty years after its publication, when Pellicer was already an established literary figure, that the book's originality was even discussed. This may be due in part to the fact that *Colores en el mar* was usually grouped with Pellicer's other early works and treated as part of his early period as a whole. It was the emphasis on Americanist themes in his subsequent works which caught the critic's eye, obscuring to some extent the linguistic originality of his first book. Only one poem from *Colores* ("Estudio") was reproduced in the controversial *Antología de la poesía mexicana moderna (Anthology of Modern Mexican Poetry)*, edited by the *Contemporáneos* group, which was so influential in the formation of the reputation of these writers.

In the enormous critical bibliography on Pellicer there are only three studies which directly and substantially speak of the book. In a recent study, the critic Porfirio Martínez Peñaloso remarked that the book's publication must have stirred no small controversy among critics of that day because of its subject matter and technical execution: "In addition to its appearance, *Colors in the Sea* must have stirred one of these facile literary storms because of its content. It contains the shortest poem that I can remember in Mexican poetry, which because of the condensation and density of the 'poetic material' rivals the *haiku*. . . . Pellicer's poem consists of one line: 'Your beauty and the sea search for my star.' The theme of the book was also unheard of. . . . Pellicer returns to the external marine world: sun, motion, and color."[8] Luis Rius, in his lengthy review of Pellicer's collected works, had earlier hinted at the book's uniqueness when he linked Pellicer's singular perception of external stimuli to the way children spontaneously respond to nature: "The ingenuous amazement of the poet and his childlike ecstasy are transformed . . . through language by means of a difficult metric game. . . . The complicated play with language attracts youthful dynamism which acts within the poet, because it offers multiple possibilities for astonishing innovations and unusual poetic creations."[9] The most penetrating observations have been made by George Melnykovich who has studied Pellicer's use of poetic diction and stressed the importance of creationist theories. Melnykovich's study constitutes the most radical departure from traditional criticism inasmuch as he draws strong and convincing parallels between Pellicer and currents of Spanish-American vanguardism. His hypothesis that the theories of the Chilean poet Vicente Huidobro were influential in the poetry of Pellicer are bolstered by the comments of the Ecuadorian poet Jorge Carrera Andrade which were made in an interview with William J. Straub: "In Latin American

poetry, the *creacionista* movement manifests itself with strong outlines. In Mexico, Venezuela, and Peru many followers of Huidobro
appear. The æsthetics of Huidobro can be identified in some poems
of Carlos Pellicer, Villaurrutia, Queremel, Parra del Riego, Alberto
Hidalgo, and others. There is no poet of the second quarter of the
XXth century who does not owe something to *creacionismo*."[10]

While he admits to the essentially polygenetic nature of many of
the techniques of vanguard art, Melnykovich states that he has
found four constants in the creationist figurative diction of Pellicer:
(1) the combination in one image of two disparate things; (2) destruction of normal spatial and temporal limitations; (3) representation of
the abstract by the concrete; and (4) the creation of unreal "sensuous" imagery.[11] In his summary statement, Melnykovich makes
some substantive remarks concerning Pellicer's relationship to the
vanguard movement as a whole and to *creacionismo* in particular:

This then is the body of the poetic work of Pellicer. A world of things,
visible and invisible, but all transformed to correspond to his unique vision
of reality. Although, as we have demonstrated, Pellicer had adopted many
of the *creacionista* techniques, philosophically there stretched a distance
between him and Huidobro. Where in Huidobro there is a tendency to
reject nature, Pellicer's relationship to nature is one of harmonious coexis-
tence. It is an interchange by which the sun, the sea, and the wind provide
him with inspiration, and he in turn dresses them in imaginative colors and
forms. . . .
Carlos Pellicer is clearly not an avant-garde artist. While he adopts many
of the devices and attitudes which originate in avant-garde movements, he
is not disposed to the avant-garde mentality.[12]

Simply stated, *Colores en el mar* is a kind of poetic potpourri
where traditional poetic conceits are mixed, at times randomly, with
unusual visual representations of the external world. The book is
neither vanguardist nor particularly traditional but rather a curious
blend of the two.

It is ironic that this first book by Pellicer was not so radically
different from the poetry of the *Contemporáneos* of the same period.
The earliest published verse of Jaime Torres Bodet, *Fervor* (*Fervor*,
1918), and *El corazón delirante* (*The Impassioned Heart*, 1922), are
characterized by a similar tone of lyric simplicity as are the short
love quatrains of Ortiz de Montellano's *Avidez* (*Avidity*, 1921), Salvador Novo's *XX Poemas* (*Twenty Poems*, 1925), and to a less

marked degree, Xavier Villaurrutia's *Reflejos* (*Reflections*, 1926). Pellicer, unlike many creative writers who have undergone radical changes in their approach to art, has not veered substantially in his poetic orientation. A boundless joy in living, an equally important identification between man and nature, as well as an admiration for hero figures emerge as essential characteristics of his verse.

CHAPTER 3

Sacrificial Stone: *The Voice of Social Concern*

I *Americanist Motifs*

THE publication in 1924 of Pellicer's second volume of verse, *Piedra de sacrificios (Sacrificial Stone)* was of decisive importance in his creative development. Bearing a prologue by the distinguished and controversial Mexican writer José Vasconcelos (1882–1952), the book marks Pellicer's entry into the arena of social concern. In a series of vibrant odes, he proclaims his faith in the future union of the Americas and glorifies its pre-Columbian heritage. Although Pellicer's overt Americanism placed him at a distance from the *Contemporáneos* group, who had now begun to move away from native themes, it was the logical result of a number of forces at work in postrevolutionary society. In the wake of the Revolution of 1910, a new wave of interest in indigenous culture was initiated. As its chief spokesman, José Vasconcelos had established a separate government program in the graphic arts which gave rise to a brilliant school of mural painters. Aided by state funds, Diego Rivera, José Clemente Orozco, and David Alfaro Siqiueros covered the facades of Mexican public buildings with epic portrayals of the struggle of the Mexican Indian.

This passionate interest in the Indian, and more broadly in indigenous culture including pre-Columbian civilization, was not unique to Mexico but was properly a Pan-American movement which began at the turn of the century with the rejection of European positivist thought by numerous intellectuals. As early as 1894, the iconoclastic Peruvian writer Manuel González-Prada (1848–1918), a champion of social reform in his country, decried the treatment of the Indian and sought to check the European-oriented ruling class. The Argentine Ricardo Rojas (1882–1957) added another dimension to the pro-Indian argument when he stressed in *Eurindia* (1924) that both

Indian and European were knit together in the New World by a mystic "force of the land." Vasconcelos himself authored the extremely influential *La raza cósmica (The Cosmic Race)* in which he preached that the destiny of the world rested with the amalgamation of all races into the fifth or cosmic race, which was to flourish in the lush Amazon river basin. Although the movement to rediscover America was based on a complex set of factors, both socioeconomic and political, it shared a number of basic denominators. Disillusioned and surfeited with European and North American models in politics and the arts, and particularly irritated with encroaching United States economic imperialism, the Latin American turned toward his own land in a quest for authenticity. Repeatedly, writers and poets stressed the uniqueness and beauty of the Latin American landscape and described in archetypal terms the Indian as a reservoir of vital energy.

It is important to note that while *La raza cósmica* was published a year after the appearance of *Piedra de sacrificios,* it was written during Vasconcelos' mission to Latin America during which Pellicer and he were in close contact. On several occasions, Pellicer has explicitly admitted the influence of Vasconcelos on his work. During an interview with this writer on June 5, 1972 and in response to a question about the influence of *La raza cósmica* on *Piedra de sacrificios,* he replied:

That's true. I met Vasconcelos under very peculiar circumstances. I was returning from my first trip to South America and I had to present a report to the Federation of Students in Mexico. I mentioned that the Central University of Caracas had been closed by the dictatorial government of General Juan Vicente Gómez, and this caused me to make strong declarations against that government while Vasconcelos, just a few weeks previously, had also uttered terrible things against the same regime in a public ceremony. This united us and made us friends, and one and a half years later he invited me to take a trip to South America, my second trip, and from this second trip came almost all of *Piedra de sacrificios.*
What did the works of Vasconcelos mean to me? Well, to a great extent, I witnessed the creation and the birth of Vasconcelos' ideas. In many matters we coincided. . . . Vasconcelos is the best writer Mexico has produced. Moreover, he is a writer of continental dimension. He is a great thinker on all the subjects of our America. However, the greatest thinker of America, the man who has exercised the most spiritual and intellectual influence in

America, is Bolívar. After Bolívar comes Sarmiento; after Sarmiento comes Martí; after Martí comes Vasconcelos. Therefore, for me, the works of Vasconcelos have been of enormous importance.

In his prologue to *Piedra de sacrificios*, Vasconcelos enumerated several of the cardinal tenets of the new Americanism, of which the chief one was a desire for Pan-American union: "Carlos Pellicer belongs to the new international family whose fatherland is the entire continent and whose race is all Spanish-speaking peoples. . . . The international family already exists and it only needs proselytes in order to cease being a sect and become a nation. . . ."[1] As he continues, Vasconcelos next refers to the importance of landscape in almost mystic terms: "Pellicer has seen his America from the air and has examined it on foot. . . . In this integral fashion he has cultivated a love for the Latin continent. A total love without reservations, like the love of a mother for her children. . . . Reading these poems I have thought of a new religion that I thought of preaching once: a religion of landscape; a devotion to external beauty, clean and grandiose, without interpretations or deformations, like language direct from divine grace. . . ."[2] In his closing remarks Vasconcelos once again reiterates the ideal of Pan-American union: "Brothers of the great, international Ibero-American family, receive this book from one of your own; keep it with love, because it contains palpitations of all the rhythms of our continental fatherland."[3]

Similar to *Colores en el mar*, *Piedra de sacrificios* is a collection of poems on various themes. The initial "Oda" ("Ode"), a microcosm of the entire book, merits close attention. The poem is a long one (some hundred lines) and might be characterized as diffuse and rambling. It begins with the classical apostrophe to the Divine (lines 1–6), a request to strengthen the force of the poet's muse: "May God's voice strengthen my cry/ may God's voice sweeten my call" ("La voz de Dios sostenga mi rugido/ . . . La voz de Dios torne dulce mi grito" [63]), which is followed (lines 7–18) by a topological survey of the principal mountains and rivers of the southern hemisphere: el Popocatépetl, el Momotombo, el Chimborazo, el Sorata, el Usumacinta, el Orinoco, etc. Lines 19–25 present a curious reference (derived directly from *La raza cósmica*) to the far Eastern origins of pre-Columbian civilization. With line 26, Pellicer repeats

the opening words of the poem and begins to stress the basic conceptual idea of the work—the pervasive influence of indigenous
culture in twentieth-century Latin America: "All the civilizations
are still in you/ and after a millennium of experience/ the hour
approaches when you will strike your horn/ The heritage of men as
strong as diamonds/ will come to fruition" ("Todas las civilizaciones
están aun en ti/ y he aquí que después desta milenaria de experien-
cia/ se acerca la hora en que van a tocar tu clarín/ Frescas herencias
de hombres de diamante/ fructificarán" [64]). After a long listing of the
heroes of Latin America, both Indian and Hispanic, he dedicates the
remainder of the poem to Rubén Darío and Simón Bolívar. The
closing lines of the poem, a supplication to Latin America to complete its cultural mission, bears a striking resemblance to later writings of Vasconcelos. This is seen above all in the image of the
airplane, which in *La raza cósmica* is pictured as an important element in cultural dissemination: "Planes fly above your cities/ obey-
ing the sweet destiny/ of the purest alliances" ("Vuelen sobre tus
ciudades/ los aviones/ obedeciendo al dulce fin/ de las alianzas más
puras" [65]).

II   *"Uxmal"*

The second poem in the book, "Uxmal," is singularly important,
since it marks one of Pellicer's earliest comments on the importance
of pre-Columbian civilization and illustrates the initiation of one of
his most characteristic techniques of treating indigenous motifs.
Simply stated, "Uxmal" is a poetic evocation of the ruins of an
ancient Mayan city located in the Yucatan Peninsula. Instead of
merely describing the physical, chromatic attributes of the ruins (as
he does elsewhere in many "portrait poems"), Pellicer narrates a
cluster of experiences related to the central image of the city from
the perspective of an omniscient poet-seer. The poem assumes
some of the characteristics of an epic hymn or vision in which the
narrator's voice is blended with a variegated pattern of exotic images
of pre-Columbian life. Thus, the central metaphorical structure of
the work appears to be associated with a subconscious or archetypal
level of creation. In the terminology of the critic Northrop Frye, we
are dealing here with that which "we vaguely describe as instinc-
tive, intuitive, inspired or involuntary."[4]

Francisco Pabón, who has carefully studied indigenous motifs in
Pellicer's poetry, considers "Uxmal" a key poem to the understand-

ing of Pellicer's world view. In a lengthy and carefully done analysis of the poem, Pabón finds a pre-Columbian prototype for "Uxmal" in the *icnocuícatl,* or "songs of sadness" of the ancient Nahuatl poets. Similar to these ancient ballads, the basic structure of "Uxmal" is related to the dramatization of a ritual act (sacrifice) and is carried out in a form of implicit dialogue. Pabón writes: "Pellicer, perhaps for the first time since pre-Columbian days, assumes the role of the poet-priest and organizes the poetic world of "Uxmal," as if it were a Nahuatl ritual hymn."[5]

A study of the poem appears to corroborate Pabón's theory. In the first ten lines the sight of the ancient ruins, triggers a sort of poetic revery in which the persona is gradually swept back through space and time. The poet responds to the physical stimulus of the view of the city by gradually moving deeper in his own consciousness until he becomes the embodiment of the spirit of Uxmal. The transition from present to past is achieved by the sixth line which contains a reference to ritual dance:

> You knock upon my heart's doors, Uxmal.
> Because of your divine emotion
> A voice is lifted up,
> And still another voice
> Uxmal.
> From high rock-summit of my heart
> Danced as for Gods danced
> Your ancient voice.

> Tocas las puertas de mi corazón,
> Uxmal.
> Por tu divina sensación
> se alza una voz,
> se alza otra voz:
> Uxmal,
> desde las rocas de mi corazón.
> Y danzó en la ruda mañana estival,
>   sacerdotal
>   tu antigua voz.[6]

(65)

The poet then enumerates a series of emotions linked to the city and its role in the sacrificial rites of pre-Columbian Mexico. The empty temples and gigantic platforms call to mind the sacrificial

aspect of Mayan religion, an idea which is further strengthened by
the repetition of the blood images a few lines below. Of particular
importance is the fusion of the poet-narrator with the physical world
of Uxmal:

> There was the terror of temples left empty
> Upon platforms gigantic;
> There was the rush, the roar
> Of bowless arrows beyond epochs,
> There was the secret faith
> Of blood-drops thick
> Which in my soul beat.
> Like trees across the twilight's curtain
> My arms uplifted
> Deep-rooted of your blood;
> The architect created symphonies
> By pompous star-routes melodic.
> The Sacred Square
> Was set by the soothsayer
> From his lookout,
> The same Square
> Where so slow my heart moved
> Then shook itself soul-free.

> Y fue el pavor de los templos vacíos
> sobre las plataformas gigantescas.
> Fueron los grandes ruidos
> de las flechas sin arco de las epocas.
> Fue la lealtad sagrada
> de las gotas espesas de tu sangre
> que se levanta en mi alma.
> Como árboles sobre el fondo de la tarde,
> mis brazos se levantaron,
> profundos, de tu sangre.
> Y fue el arquitecto sinfonizante
> de melodías y rumbos de astros,
> jugador de serpientes entre el muro,
> florista en el tibor.
> Y fue la plaza sagrada
> obtenida por el adivino
> desde su mirador.
> Aquella plaza donde mi corazón
> fue a pasos lentos
> y se sacó del alma. . . .

(66)

Lines 12–24 present three allusive images which draw in and focus on the concept of divinity by the use of successively smaller things: an "architect" of the heavens, a snake charmer, and a sacred flower jar. The last sentence (lines 25–27) is a description of the city's plaza, the site of the mystical experience of the poet presented in the next part of the poem (lines 28–41).

Approximately from lines 34–41, the narrator shifts from describing the magnitude of the city to a depiction of the effects of the temple on his own poetic sensibility. Past and present fuse in a moment of poetic truth, an instant of suspended time.

The poet is also aware of his own smallness and unimportance in the universe when he represents his soul as an atom (line 33) and an ant (line 34). This suspension of time is a productive period (line 31), because it gives rise to this poem, which the poet's soul sings:

> Ant, betwixt blocks of centuries,
> My soul suspended here,
> The tragic quiet of you
> Twixt merry instant triste moment.
> From the House of the Soothsayer
> I tossed off then drank down
> Religions like a winecup.

> Hormiga entre bloques de siglos,
> alma mía que suspendiste
> la quietud trágica de tus movimentos
> entre el instante alegre el momento triste.
> Desde la casa del adivino
> disfruté de todas las religiones
> como de una copa de vino.

> (66)

The allusion to suspended animation reinforces the extravisionary posture of the narrator, making the poem more plausible to the reader. It was as if Pellicer, the poet of the twentieth century, had for a moment seen the ruins of Uxmal through the eyes of his ancient counterpart. The poem concludes with approximately the same lines with which it began, an indication that the dream is over and the poet has returned to the present.

> You knocked upon my heart's doors
> Uxmal.
> A voice is lifted up,
> And still another voice.

Uxmal,
Divine emotion.

Tu tocaste la puerta de mi corazón,
Uxmal;
se alza una voz,
se oye otra voz.
Uxmal,
es tu divina sensación.

                                                              (67)

The same identification between the poet and his indigenous past
is seen in "Iguazú," a description of the waterfall of the same name
on the Argentine-Brazilian border. As in "Oda" and "Uxmal," Pellicer extols the beauties of his native America and proclaims again
the second coming of the Indian race: "Powerful and terrible waters/
Your thunder is the message/ of the dead races to the great living
race/ which will build in its youth a pyramid/ of civil renovation"
("Agua poderosa y temible,/ tu trueno es el mensaje/ de las razas
muertas a la gran raza viva/ que alzará en años jóvenes la pirámide
de las renovaciones cívicas" [67]). The poet sees in the waterfall's
ceaseless motion a dynamic force with which he tries to identify:
"Waters of Iguazú, great waters, proud waters/ my will shall be like
yours/ melodious and spirited" ("Agua grande, agua soberbia/ mi
voluntad será como la tuya/ numerosa y fanática" [68]).

III Travel Poems

With the exception of these initial poems, which set the tone for
the collection, it is best to consider the remainder of *Piedra de
sacrificios* under two broad categories: travel and social protest.
Under the first heading, it is possible to identify a number of selections which are purely descriptive pieces. The most outstanding
selections in this grouping are the four poems which comprise the
"Suite Brasilera, Poemas aéreos" ("Brazil Suite, Aerial Poems"). As
in "Estudio," Pellicer at times attempts to defy the norms of poetic
perspective by giving the reader a sense of spatial distance between
himself and what is narrated in the poem. Here, for example, Pellicer evokes an aerial image of Rio de Janeiro:

From the plane,
the panoramic orchestra of Rio de Janeiro
sounds in my heart.

From the crest of Corcovado
to the waves of Copacabana
happiness is a simple distance that has passed
blurring the nearest dates with its silvery hands.
I'll bind my starry existence
to the divine rock of Pao de Acucar
which sees the bursting dawn sooner than the ocean waters. . . .[7]

Desde el avión,
la orquesta panorámica de Río de Janeiro
se escucha en mi corazón.
Desde la cumbre del Corcovado
hasta las olas de Copacabana,
la dicha es una simple distancia que ha pasado
borrando fechas próximas con sus manos plateadas.
Ataré mi existencia sideral
a la divina roca del Pao de Assucar
que ve nacer la aurora antes que el agua mar. . . .

(78)

It is important to note that reality here appears not to be described but rather re-created through a collage of traditional and nontraditional poetic conceits. One particularly telling technical feature of the poem is Pellicer's propensity to relate one artistic medium to another. Thus, in the first two lines of the poem, the kaleidoscopic visual pattern of Río from the air is compared to the multiple notes and chords of an orchestra. The motif extends throughout the poem, giving it a unity of tone and feeling.

Another important feature of the descriptive poems in *Piedra de sacrificios* is the repeated effort by the poet to establish a pantheistic identification between man and nature. Much like "Iguazú," where Pellicer saw in the "Savage waters of a Mexico" a reservoir of vital energy, in "La nieve" ("The Snow"), his spirit becomes transfixed at the sight of the grandeur of the Andes mountains:

Aconcagua marks its seven thousand meter-might
While Tupungato's brutal face smiles down;
The landscape adjoins worlds beyond.
Across my shaken soul
In nakedness defile
The Andes, space-magic which is life.[8]

Sus siete mil metros vierte el Aconcagua
y en su facha brutal sonríe el Tupungato.
El paisaje se conecta con otros mundos.
Sobre mi alma un poco destruida
pasa el desfile desnudo
de los Andes y el vuelo mágico de la vida.

(70)

IV *Poems of Protest*

The poems in *Piedra de sacrificios* which are concerned with Pellicer's denunciation of contemporary social evils have received the most critical attention. In many cases, his references to social reality—above all, Yankee imperialism—take the form of asides or loosely connected interjections. Such is the case in "Divagación del puerto" ("Port Digression"), a kind of potpourri of recollections of his trip to Colombia by way of the United States and Cuba. Here he states his dislike for New York City and whimsically declares that in Veracruz "There are many sharks/ who frequently eat Yankees" ("En Veracruz hay muchos tiburones/ que comen yanquis con frecuencia" [76]). In "Cuba," Pellicer laments the encroachment of the United States: "The cynical, brutal Yankee/ strangled you with his hygienic hand" ("Te estranguló con mano higiénica/ el yanqui cínico y brutal" [88]) and in "Elegía" ("Elegy"), he projects much the same concern for Mexico: "With their phonographs and thieves' hands/ their modest religion and their catalogs/ organized by a dentist/ the barbarians will come . . ." ("Con sus fonógrafos y sus manos ladronas/ su religión modesta y sus catálogos,/ y organizados por un dentista/ vendrán los bárbaros" [90]). The bitter caricature of the United States as a sinister exploiter appears again in "Historia" ("History"). The poem, which begins with a biblical citation, "Blessed are those who suffer for they will be comforted," is centered around an apparent dream experience in which Pellicer fantacizes a meeting with Christ. His contempt for the United States is apparent even here as he describes a Yankee tycoon telling Christ he will pay him a huge sum for a recording of his voice. However, in the majority of these poems, his treatment of the problem of United States economic imperialism is characterized by a deadly seriousness. "A Germán Arciniegos" ("To Germán Arciniegas") is a case in point. Here, Pellicer again demonstrates his predilection for tactile imagery: "My America/ I touch you on the raised map/ atop my favorite desk"

("América mía/ te palpo en el mapa de relieve/ que está sobre mi mesa predilecta" [73]). The sight of the outlines of the Latin American republics then leads the poet to decry foreign exploitation. The poem closes pessimistically, an atypical feature of Pellicer's poetry: "I touch you with both my hands/ and when I am about to tell you everything/ I become a sea of tears" ("Te palpo con mis dos manos,/ y cuando voy a decírtelo todo,/ me vuelvo un cielo de lágrimas" [74]).

The theme of economic exploitation again appears in the "Balada trágica del corazón" ("The Tragic Ballad of the Heart"). The poet meditates on the destiny of the Americas as he stands on the same battleground in Venezuela where Simón Bolívar once fought: "Lands of America strangled by the despot/ or by the Yankee/ technical leader of dishonor" ("Tierras de América estranguladas por los déspotas,/ o por el yanqui,/ líder técnico del deshonor" [84]).

The most technically complex and significant protest poem in *Piedra de sacrificios* is the three-part narrative poem, "Oda a Cuauhtémoc" ("Ode to Cuauhtémoc"). Cuauhtémoc, the nephew of Montezuma and the last of the Aztec emperors, is next to Simón Bolívar one of Pellicer's favorite hero figures. Cuauhtémoc—a Nahuatl name meaning "Falling Eagle"—had already been established by the Peruvian poet José Santos Chocano as a symbol of Indian suffering at the hands of the European. Chroniclers of the conquest have attested to the stoic heroism the young emperor displayed at the hands of the Spaniards who tortured and hanged him after the siege of Tenochtitlán.

It is appropriate here to suspend our chronological approach in order to study the "Oda a Cuauhtémoc" in the context in which it most recently appeared. In 1962, Pellicer published three groups of poems relating to the Cuauhtémoc legend under the title *Con palabras y fuego (With Words and Fire)*. The book opens with the three-part ode which first appeared in *Piedra de sacrificios*. It is prefaced by an apostrophe-sonnet to Christ in which the poet elicits his intervention on behalf of the disillusioned and disheartened peoples of America. After establishing an elegiac tone in this prefatory poem, Pellicer shifts perspective in the first thematic division by moving from Christian religious symbols to an area of pre-Hispanic mythological reference. In the first stanza, the poet addresses the fallen Cuauhtémoc and declares that his tragedy is still perceptible; the injustice of his death is so overwhelming that the poet feels obliged to "go about shouting, proclaiming your greatness." The second stanza describes the fall of the Aztec empire which, in the hands of Cuauhtémoc, "fell like a wounded eagle" and foretells the coming of the Spaniard. After placing the tragic figure of Cuauhtémoc within the framework of Aztec cosmology, the third stanza returns to the present and the poet bemoans the tragedy of contemporary times, for now the oppression of the Spaniard has been replaced by the economic imperialism of the United States:

> And all vain, absurd America
> is putrifying
> Oh, destiny of the relentless tragedy!
> No one will be able to stop you
> You will burn our feet again with fire
> You will come with your brutal hands
> from the land of the mediocre, ordered, corpulent Yankee
> You will come with the din of machinery,
> to rob, to kill, to buy our leaders with your great wealth.

> Toda nuestra América vanidosa y absurda
> se está pudriendo.
> ¡Oh destino de la tragedia inexorable y gigantesca!
> ¿Nadie podrá detenerte?
> ¿Volverás a ponernos las plantas en el fuego?
> ¿Vendrás con tus manos brutales
> del país de los yanquis, mediocre, ordenado y corpulento?
> ¿Vendrás entre estallidos y máquinas
> a robar, a matar, a comprar caciques con tu inacabable dinero?

(97)

Apart from the tendency to examine the socioeconomic problems of modern Mexico within the context of pre-Hispanic myth, there is another significant facet to this poem. Pellicer employs a device which becomes predominant in his later works: the transformation of the persona into various forms of the natural world. Thus, in the first stanza, we read: "Your proud, young heroism/ change me, from the leaf I am/ into mountain and forest" ("Y tu juventud heróica y soberbia/ me tornan/ de hoja que soy/ en montaña y selva" [95]). The narrator does not limit himself to describing the physical world but becomes an active participant in it. It is this aspect of his work which has led some critics to speak of Pellicer as a mystic or pantheist.

This initial "Oda a Cuauhtémoc" is followed in *Con palabras y fuego* by an untitled poem, dated Chapultepec, 1944, originally published in the book *Subordinaciones* (*Subordinations,* 1949) with the title "Poema en tiempo vegetal" ("Poem in Vegetable Time"). In the first four of the poem's twelve stanzas, the poet describes his entrance into a lush tropical forest where the distinctions between the narrator and the world about him soon become blurred. The rays of the tropical sun which he feels "sonorously in body and soul" appear to generate a transformation. In the middle of the second stanza, he declares, "I'm singing among the trees/ and in the foliage of my voice/ nature's birds nibble" ("Y estoy cantando entre los árboles/ y en el follaje de mi voz/ pican los pájaros del viento" [411]). In the sixth stanza, the poetic persona addresses the tragic hero Cuauhtémoc who is presented as a symbol of emerging Mexico: "Handsome, strong trees/ the men of Mexico/ Some day will be like these trees" (¡Hermosos y fuertes árboles!/ como estos árboles han de ser un día/ en México, los hombres" [413]). In the last stanza, Pellicer unites the figure of *hombre-árbol* ("man-tree") and the land through a fertility image. Thus, like the rain which enriches the earth, the words of the poet unite with matter and blossom in creative harmony.

Con palabras y fuego closes with a long, three-part poem, dated Tepoztlán, June, 1962. The depiction of the death and resurrection of Cuauhtémoc becomes a curious blend of indigenous and Christian religious symbols. Sonja Karsen put it best, when she wrote: "In *Con palabras y fuego,* Cuauhtémoc assumes Christlike proportions and appears as the redeemer of the Mexican people, at the precise moment when they are ready to emulate the achievements of the past, in order to fulfill their destiny which will ultimately lead to freedom and prosperity for all."[9]

Some summary comments on the importance of *Piedra de sacrificios* are in order. In the first place, and in spite of the dim view most critics have taken of it, the book was enormously important in establishing Pellicer's reputation as a poet. In an important review article,[10] the well-known Nobel laureate, Gabriela Mistral, dubbed Pellicer the Poet of America and warmly praised him for rediscovering America's indigenous past. Her comments, together with the considerable prestige of Vasconcelos' backing, no doubt contributed to Pellicer's early recognition. In terms of the political and social climate of the times—emerging nationalism, Pan-Americanism—it is easy to see how the book found an audience. It might be pointed out that in the same year that the book was published, Víctor Raúl Haya de la Torre (1895–) founded the important pro-Indian political party, The Popular Alliance for American Revolution, which influenced the dissemination of information concerning the racial equality and cultural achievements of the native American.

The question of Pellicer's relation to the indigenous literature of the 1920s and the literary merit of his early poetry is a complex issue and cannot be explained in absolutes. While on the one hand, *Piedra de sacrificios* evinces a debt to the pro-Indian political milieu of the era, it is not entirely a work of literary propaganda. To the contrary, in spite of its rhetorical penchant and missionary zeal, the book is a work of synthesis, a careful blending of ideology and aesthetics. Francisco Pabón, one of the few critics who have recognized the importance of the collection, dedicates two chapters in his study on Pellicer to this subject. From the point of view of poetic technique, *Piedra de sacrificios* is important because it marks the earliest use of what we might call "ritualistic form" in Pellicer's verse, while on a thematic plane its significance derives from the introduction of important pre-Hispanic hero figures.

CHAPTER 4

A Return to the Simple Life:
Six, Seven Poems

I A Change in Direction

THE same year in which he published *Piedra de sacrificios* (1924), Pellicer came out with *6, 7 poemas*, which in many ways might be considered the conceptual opposite of the former. Luis Rius aptly characterized them as the "Night and day of the poet. Sun and shadow."[1] In contrast to *Piedra de sacrificios*, *6, 7 poemas* signaled a surprising return to more simple themes and techniques. Discursive hyperbole and epic eloquence gave way to extended lyricism, simple statement, and verbal economy. In many ways, *6, 7 poemas* marks the poetic continuation and refinement of *Colores en el mar*.

This collection of twenty-eight poems begins, much like *Colores en el mar*, with a brief affirmation of the poet's faith in human destiny. This initial poem in many ways is reminiscent of the modernist poet Rubén Darío's "Canción de otoño en primavera" ("Autumn Song in Spring"), although here the theme of youth has become more stylized with reference to the Muses, the nine sister goddesses in Greek mythology who presided over song and poetry. There is also an important sensuous image in the third line where the poet exclaims that he dominates and fully controls the life force. This is juxtaposed to a reference to death:

> Divine youth, golden crown,
> window to paradise.
> I possess you completely! (Death doesn't figure in my thoughts)
> Listen to what the Muses sing:
> light the night, destiny has died.

> ¡Divina juventud, corona de oro,
> ventana al paraíso.

Te poseo total! (La muerte no figura en el reparto íntimo.)
Oíd lo que cantan las musas:
enciende la noche, ha muerto el destino.

(101)

There is considerable thematic variety in 6, 7 *poemas;* landscapes,
love poems, and autocritical pieces all are loosely linked by a dis-
tinctly cultivated lyric exuberance. Much as in *Colores en el mar,*
the poet seems to be deliberately straining the limits of language to
evoke impressions of newness, freshness, and vitality. "Primavera"
("Spring") appears in many ways to be an elongation of some of
Pellicer's earlier descriptive poems. The poem, which consists of
fifty-four lines, was dedicated to the Nicaraguan poet Salomón de la
Selva (1893–1959), who wrote poems both in English *(Tropical
Town and Other Poems)* and in Spanish *(El soldado desconocido, La
ilustre familia).* Here Pellicer's fundamental technique entails the
use of questions directed to Salomón with replies by a personified
Spring. The poem's initial verses (lines 1–13) evoke a feeling of
building enthusiasm underscored by the use of the subjunctive
mood as the poetic narrator addresses the Nicaraguan poet. This
conventionalized introduction gives way in lines 14–50 to a gradual
accretion of disparate images of spring. In the last four lines the poet
shifts his focus back to Salomón by appending a puzzling closing:
"I'll send you 10 minutes of this afternoon/ for your collection of
paintings" ("Te mando 10 minutos de esta tarde/ para tu colección
de acuarelas" [103]).

II *"Dawn"*

As in his earlier verse, Pellicer continues the tendency to elaborate visual images. In "Aurora" ("Dawn"), he addresses the personified morning light with a series of flashy color conceits. Dawn is not
depicted as the classic goddess of the morning sun, but rather as a
uniquely Mexican deity whose early rays are linked to the Mexican
landscape through a series of chromatic impressions. The poem
begins with a simile in which the arrival of dawn is related to personified areas of the Mexican landscape in lines 1–3. This is followed in
lines 4–5 by an enumeration of Mexican place names: Pátzcuaro, a
scenic lake in the state of Michoacán; Chapala, a lake in the state of
Jalisco; Tzintzuntzan, a city near lake Pátzcuaro rich in pre-

Columbian artifacts; and Uruapan and Oaxaca, picturesque Mexican colonial cities.

In line six, the poet-narrator directly addresses the personified dawn, thus altering the poem's narrative perspective. What had begun as a description of Dawn's arrival now becomes a kinetic portrait of the Mexican landscape. It is a world of dancing palm trees and flying clouds where the moon has become Dawn's "white umbrella." As the poem draws to a close, the reader is left with a multifaceted portrait of Dawn based on unusual linkages and associations. This abstract picture is concretized somewhat in the last seven lines of the poem with specific references to the "knees of springtime," Dawn's "tinted feet" and "smile." The poem is an unusual variation on a very traditional theme:

> Dawn came
> as in the chocolate bowl of Uruapan
> and upon Oaxaca's shawl.
> Yuridiapúndaro and Pátzcuaro!
> Tzintzuntzan and Chapala.
> Do you recall the blue stag
> your glances painted?
> Bring light, draw it nearer,
> until all shadows have been forgotten.
> The green wave that toppled
> over the empty shore
> lost its foam cargo
> in the white of your lilies. . . .[2]

> Amaneció,
> como en la jícara de Uruapan
> y en el sarape de Oaxaca.
> Yuridiapúndaro y Pátzcuaro!
> Tzintzuntzan y Chapala.
> ¿Recordáis el venado azul
> que vuestras miradas pintaron?
> Traed, acercad la luz,
> todas las sombras se olvidaron.
> La ola verde que encalló
> sobre el litoral vacío
> perdió su cargamento de espuma
> por culpa de vuestros lirios.

(106)

III   *Nature Poems*

There are a number of nature portraits like "Aurora" which manifest a repeated tendency to depict man infused with nature: "Motivos" ("Motives"), "Scherzo," "Sembrador" ("Sower"), and "Segador" ("Reaper") are among the most outstanding examples of this technique. "Motivos" exemplifies Pellicer's ability to evoke a complex series of visual images within a controlled poetic framework. Here the central thematic and imagistic motifs imaginatively call forth a feeling of reverent wonder as the poet gradually constructs a portrait of the pleasures of the bucolic life. The poem is composed of two stanzas of irregular length. In the opening lines Pellicer makes an immediate association between man and nature through a tripart visual image linking a plowman to his oxen who in turn are related to the dawn. Thus the level of metaphoric illusion becomes gradually more abstract as the poet moves from man to animal to nature concretized. This interpenetration between man and nature is further heightened by a series of fertility images in which the plowman is depicted as an archetypal figure of creation. His hands are "red" and "potent," his sweat "sacred," and he is capable of sowing "faith" in the furrows he plows. The poem comes full circle in the last stanza where the impressions of creativity are replaced with allusions to completion. The plowman who cast the spores of life in the first stanza emerges here as the biblical shepherd and symbolic guardian of life.

"Segador" and "Sembrador" are two tightly constructed visual poems. In both cases, the central poetic image is derived from a linking of two levels of reality: the world of man and the greater physical universe of which he is a part. Both poems caught the eye of the poetess Gabriela Mistral who reproduced them in an early note on Pellicer's poetry first published in *El Mercurio* in Chile and then reprinted in the prestigious *Repertorio Americano*.

"Segador" exemplifies well this interplay between man and nature. The poem, dedicated to José Vasconcelos, consists of four stanzas. Similar to "Motivos" it is developed around a central metaphoric image: here the comparison between man and nature with an implicit analogy between reaper and poet. There is also evident a clear attempt to describe one medium in terms of another. Thus the opening of the poem depicts the reaper rhythmically cutting the golden stalks of grain which are compared to the afternoon sun:

The harvester rhythmically
Reaps the afternoon.
His sickle is so fine.
He reaps the sweet grain-spikes and he reaps the afternoon.

El segador, con pausas de música,
segaba la tarde.
Su hoz es tan fina,
que siega las dulces espigas y siega la tarde.

(135)

In the second stanza the auditory and musical dimension is stressed again as the sickle becomes the reaper's "sharpened noise":

Reaper walking through golden fields.
With his sharpened noise,
Laying waste the fine heights of gold
Also casts the twilight down.

Segador que en dorados niveles camina
con su ruido afilado,
derrotando las finas alturas de oro
echa abajo también el ocaso.

(135)

In the final two stanzas the reaper emerges as a figure of cosmic proportions whose physical stature now has been fused with the optical forces of daylight and sunset. There again appears a reference to music which may perhaps be thought of in terms of the rhythmic forces of nature.

He cut the blades of wheat.
His pause was music.
His shadow lengthened the afternoon.
In his eyes shone a light
Which at times
Danced all over the landscape.

Segaba las claras espigas.
Su pausa era música.
Su sombra alargaba la tarde.
En los ojos traía un lucero
que a veces
brincaba por todo el paisaje.

(135)

The "Sembrador" is an almost parallel development of the same theme. Here, however, the central metaphor of sower as poet may be more easy to perceive. The sower here clearly achieves messianic attributes, for we are told that he sows the dawn and that the sun grows from his magical hands. The poem climaxes with a forceful intermixture of man and nature:

> He sowed the land
> His step was beautiful: neither short nor long
> The mountains danced in his eyes
> and all the landscape in his arms.

> Sembraba la tierra
> Su paso era bello: ni corto ni largo.
> En sus ojos cabían los montes
> y todo el paisaje en sus brazos.
>
> (134)

While the verse of 6, 7 *poemas* continues to be developed with nature imagery, the purely descriptive portrait-poems of the earlier collections have given way to pieces in which the poet attempts some analysis of his thoughts and feelings. Love, for example, is a theme in several poems such as "La noche" ("The Night") and "Soledades" ("Solitudes"). In the former, the poet longs for the absent lover and, continuing his propensity to concretize the abstract, presents her memory with tactile detail:

> In the midst of the desert of your absence,
> I lean on your memory
> As on the trunk of a palm tree. . . .

> En mitad del desierto de tu ausencia,
> me reclino en tu recuerdo
> como en el talle de una palmera. . . .
>
> (104)

In "Soledades," Pellicer again develops the theme of longing for the absent lover. The poem is more tightly organized than "La Noche" and consists of seven recollections, each prefaced by the statement, "recuerdo" ("I remember"). What makes the poem unique is that the attributes of the beloved are almost always described in terms of natural phenomena: "The lightning of your glance" ("el relámpago de tus propias miradas"); "the moonlight nights of your eyes" ("noches de luna de tus ojos"); "the dawn of your hands" ("crepúsculo de tus manos"); and "your body is mahogany" ("tu cuerpo es de caoba"). In "Solitudes," Pellicer projects a correspondence between man and nature through the figure of an absent lover. The linking between man and nature continues and achieves greater significance in his later poetry.

In the poem, "Noche," the love motif appears again. This time, however, the poet focuses on the recollection of an exhilarating moment shared by him and his beloved. The memory of a tropical storm becomes the point of departure for a meditation on the cosmic harmony of the universe. In the last stanza, through an association of plant images, the poet implies that his love like the vegetation which surrounds him was nurtured by the life-giving tropical rain:

> Because of this moment, I shall girdle myself
> Laurel, thorn, hands, flowers
> renewing, succumbing
> through the victory of love.

> Por ese instante he de ceñirme,
> laurel, espina, manos, flor,
> resucitando y sucumbiendo
> por la victoria del amor.

(130)

IV Reflections on Poetry

There are several other nostalgic love poems, among them "Aniversario" ("Anniversary") and "Nocturno" ("Nocturne"), but the most singular treatment of the theme is "Canto del amor perfecto" ("Song of Perfect Love"). The love Pellicer describes here is neither erotic nor romantic but rather a platonic love for Christ. It is interesting to note that Pellicer again employs nature imagery to delineate the figure of Christ. His hands are described as: "a little water with moonlight" ("tus manos son un poco de agua/ con luna") and his voice issues from "hazy dawns" (albas oscuras). As in later poems, the moon and the sun become pictorial representations of divine energy: "Your eyes open in the night/ and your last glance/ closes the slow circles of dawn" ("Tus ojos se abren en la noche/ y tu última mirada/ cierra los lentos círculos del alba" [114]).

In several poems in this collection, Pellicer meditates about his
own involvement in the act of writing poetry. More than philosophic
poems, they are stylized impressions of his art. In "Elegía"
("Elegy"), for example, he underscores his desire to express himself
with colors rather than words. "Elegía" is an excellent example of
Pellicer's virtuosity as a poet, for here—as opposed to his purely
visual poems—he is able to establish a link of tone and mood between poet and reader. Dedicated to "Nobody," the poem builds to
a gradual dramatic climax. In the first fifteen lines Pellicer heaps
staccato images of ennui one upon the other in an effort to underscore his sense of futility and boredom. The poet stares into empty
streets, thinks of his absent lover, his hatred of books and sunless
days. Even here in a seemingly conventional, confessional framework, unusual images and associations appear. The poet muses that
the cathedral looks "mortgaged" and that he feels as if he has eaten
"Yankee apples." From line 16 to line 39, passive reflection, however, erupts into an extended exclamation as the poet passionately
expresses a desire to express himself with color rather than words:

> If I were a painter
> I would save myself.
> With color I would create an entire civilization.
> Blue would be red
> And orange,
> grey
> Green would leap out as stupendous blacks
> Wisdom of new colors!
>
> Si yo fuera pintor,
> me salvaría.
> Con el color
> toda una civilización yo crearía.
> El azul sería
> rojo
> y el anaranjado,
> gris;
> el verde saltaría en negros estupendos.
> ¡Sabidurías
> de los colores nuevos!

(119)

Lines 27–33 echo the Americanist motifs of *Piedra de sacrificios*
with an enumeration of the geological wonders of Spanish-American

mountain peaks: Tunguragua and el Sajama. The entire meditation concludes with an important sensory image: "I would have eyes in my hands" ("Yo tendría ojos en mis manos"). This telling allusion to a correspondence among the senses foretells an important tendency in Pellicer's poetry to depict poetry as a multisensory phenomenon.

"Nocturno" ("Nocturne") would seem to be the epilogue for *Piedra de sacrificios*, for here Pellicer stresses that he is tired of dealing with tragic, somber themes and wants to sing again the joys of living, symbolized through bright visual images (sun, dawn) suggestive of hope and rebirth:

> Change your melancholy expression,
> climb your Andes, plant your flag,
> and make your sad oak tree a ship
> filling its sails in the spring sun.

> Muda tu gesto aciago,
> sube tus Andes, planta tu bandera,
> y haz de tu roble triste la nave de honda quilla
> que embandere de sol la primavera.

>   (126)

In yet another poem entitled "Nocturno," Pellicer assumes an autocritical posture and laments that he is a passionate being incapable of close scrutiny and careful meditation:

> I don't have time to look at things
> As I would like to.
> They just glide across my face
> And all I see are radio-addressed profound corners
> . . . .
> I live on a gilded periphery; not enjoying the central pleasure
> of things. Unfolding golden centuries in my soul. . . .

> No tengo tiempo de mirar las cosas
> como yo lo deseo.
> Se me escurren sobre la mirada
> y todo lo que veo
> son esquinas profundas rotuladas con radio
> . . . .
> Vivo en doradas márgenes; ignoro el central gozo
> de las cosas. Desdoblo siglos de oro en mi ser.

>   (131)

This autocritical tendency culminates in "Deseos" ("Desires"), one of Pellicer's best-known works and the quintessential poem of 6, 7 poemas. Here Pellicer laments that he is merely a colorist poet and requests that he be allowed to write more introspective verse. The poem is a short one (twenty lines) in which the narrator directs his voice to a personified embodiment of nature (the tropics) and laments that he is unable to express deeply felt emotions, that he is merely a superficial colorist poet. Structurally, "Deseos" is a good example of Pellicer's tendency to make adaptations or shifts of focus within seemingly conventional forms. The initial use of an apostrophe, a figure of speech in which something is addressed as though it were living, is of course not by itself a startling device and may set up in the mind of the experienced reader of poetry a degree of anticipation for traditional tropes and stylized poetic diction. However, this initial question elicits no answer from personified nature, but rather is gradually transformed in the closing verses of the poem into a soulful cry. There are important imagistic and thematic links here with poems such as "Elegía." The first four lines, in particular, call to mind the recurrent association between the senses (above all tactile and visual) which seem to be ever present in Pellicer's verse. In short, the opening lines have a dual importance: they demonstrate a very effective way of establishing a bond between narrator and reader (achieved here through the almost auditory intimacy of the second person form) and show how adept Pellicer is at translating an emotional experience through the medium of a graphic, visual image:

> Tropics, why did you give me
> these hands brimming with color?
> Whatever I touch
> brims over with sunlight.[3]

> Trópico, para que me diste
> las manos llenas de color.
> Todo lo que yo toque
> se llenara de sol.

> (123)

In lines 5–16 the poet continues to stress the synesthetic nature of poetic experience with images such as "sound of a glass sunflower." More importantly, however, he alludes to a process of transformation by which the narrator is described in terms usually applied to flora and fauna. Thus the persona declares that he will travel through distant lands like a sunflower, that he will soak up light, and that he yearns to be strewn about like the petals of a flower. Similarly significant is the parallel use of the interjection ("Let me!") in lines 7–8 to underscore the building dramatic tension of the poem:

> I'll pass through the delicate afternoons of other lands
> with the sound of a glass sunflower.
> Let me for one moment
> stop being all noise and color.
> Let me for one moment
> change the climate of my heart,
> soak up the half-light of some solitary thing,
> lean out from a distant balcony in silence,
> sink deep into the fine folds of my cloak,
> be strewn upon the bank of a quiet passion,
> softly caress the long delicate hair of women
> and write my reflections out with a fine pencil.

> En las tardes sutiles de otras tierras
> pasaré con mis ruidos de vidrio tornasol.
> Déjame un solo instante
> dejar de ser grito y color.
> Déjame un solo instante
> cambiar de clima el corazón,
> beber la penumbra de una cosa desierta,
> inclinarme en silencio sobre un remoto balcón,
> ahondarme en el manto de pliegues finos,
> dispersarme en la orilla de una suave devoción,
> acariciar dulcemente las cabelleras lacias
> y escribir con un lápiz muy fino mi meditación.

> (123)

"Deseos" climaxes with a four-line exclamation in which the poet returns to the initial question which began the poem. Quite apart from the obvious structural unity which this technique bestows on the poem, it should be pointed out that "Deseos" is among the shorter, more carefully constructed poems in this book. It represents aesthetically a balance of theme and form, for there is a feeling of symmetry and balance present which is lacking in many of the other compositions. As we have seen, "Deseos" begins with a question (lines 1–2) which is gradually transformed in the closing verses into a soulful exclamation. On a metaphoric level as well, Pellicer has been more successful in controlling his use of poetic language, since the central poetic image remains clear and intelligible.

This identification between nature and poetry is developed in a number of other poems: "Al dejar un alma" ("Upon Leaving a Soul"), "Dame, oh bosque" ("Oh Give me Forest"), and "Nocturno" ("Nocturne"). In the first, Pellicer establishes a relationship between water and poetic inspiration with the insinuation that his emotions have been moved by the forces of nature: "I joined my thought to your somber joys/ I tasted the sweetness of your slow words" ("Alié mi pensamiento a tus goces sombríos/ y gusté la dulzura de tus palabras lentas" [113]). In the second, similar to "Deseos," he directly addresses nature (the forest) and asks her to give the *mot juste* for which he searches: "Sow my solitude with brightness and song/ make me hear the word I want in the shade" ("Siembra mi soledad de luceros y cánticos/ y hazme oír en la sombra la palabra que quiero" [128]). Finally, in "Nocturno," nature is not only depicted as a source of poetic inspiration but as refuge and haven for the poet: "Peace is winter's greenery/ you will find peace in Spring" ("La paz es fronda del invierno./ Tu en primavera tendrás paz" [132]).

Critically, *6, 7 poemas* is an important, if not enigmatic, book. At a very early stage in Pellicer's career, it shows a fixation with the problem of the creative act as an objective phenomenon as well as general movement towards restraint in form and content. It is not unusual that this was the collection which received the earliest critical attention from his colleagues. For example, a number of poems were anthologized in the controversial *Antología de la poesía mexicana moderna* (1928), edited by Jorge Cuesta in collaboration with other members of the *Contemporáneos* group.

Although in general terms (and certainly in contrast to *Piedra de sacrificios*) *6, 7 poemas* may be described as "conventional" in terms of poetic technique, the book is by no means entirely traditional. "Scherzo" typifies this duality. The title, which is a musical term referring to a humorous instrumental composition or movement usually executed in quick triple time, is clearly indicative of the poet's attitude toward his work. The thirty-one-line poem might be best described as a series of stylized impressions of the seashore which are joined together by the repetition at the beginning of successive verses of the conjunction "and." In lines 1–7 the reader's eye is mentally guided by a rapid enumeration of visual impressions. The poet begins by focusing on the gilded surface of the sea, then moving on to the sands of the shore, to the feet, and finally to the naked body of a swimmer. Lines 8–12 describe the abstract feelings of "sweetness" and "freshness" that this seascape evokes as a totality in the mind of the poet. Suddenly, in line 24, the poet registers a radical change in outlook. The single line exclamation: "And a shout" ("Y un grito") serves to introduce a complex series of apparently unrelated images:

> And a shout
> a poorly sketched woman carrying a fish
> Like an ad for a jewelry store.
> And the incredible skill of the waves
> which ought to win the Nobel Prize
> for physical education. . . .
>
> Y una mujer desdibujada que lleva un pez
> y así parece anuncio de joyerías.
> Y la destreza imponderable de las olas
> que bien merece ya el premio Nobel
> por cultura física. . . .

                                                                    (121)

This sudden shift in tone and mood, the insertion of nontraditional language within an otherwise normative poem, is a characteristic of Pellicer's verse which we have seen earlier. In a perceptive essay, Andrew Debicki explained the effects of his sudden shift of perspective in this poem: "The joking allusion to the Nobel Prize, the personification of waves as athletes, and the modern image of a jewelry store advertisement call attention to themselves and break the previous mood. They also help the reader accept the viewpoint of the speaker; the latter turns out to be not a sentimental admirer of conventional seascapes, but a modern man possessed of a sense of humor, who can perceive unusual correspondences and who can even parody his previous outlook. Thanks to this change, the theme of nature's beauty and its effects on man has become more credible and more exciting."[4]

In summary it might be said that if *Piedra de sacrificios* helped identify Pellicer with emergent Pan-Americanism, *6, 7 poemas* was instrumental in establishing his reputation among other poets. It is a book of startling modernity. In such key poems as "Deseos," "Elegía," and "Scherzo," Pellicer continued and refined a number of poetic techniques begun in *Colores en el mar*. There is a noticeable and constant effort in these poems to present conventional themes from an unusual linguistic and narrative perspective. The most pointed comments about *6, 7 poemas* were made by Alfredo Roggiano: "Around 1924, when ultraism was triumphing in America, Pellicer succeeded with *6, 7 poemas* not only in establishing the metaphor and image as the essential components of poetry, but opened the way so that the young Mexican poets could once again in Mexico, in all America, be confident of the poetic gifts of the New World. . . ."[5] Here Roggiano stresses the essentially synthetic originality of this book: the topographical and geographical wonders of the New World are presented through poetic forms which, while innovative, were still comprehensible. It was as if Pellicer had distilled some of the vanguardist techniques into a more genuinely American form of expression.

CHAPTER 5

The Transplanted Tropics:
One Twenty

THE fruition of Pellicer's travel experiences in Europe and the
Near East, *Hora y veinte (One Twenty)*, was published in Paris
in 1927. An interesting glimpse into the genesis of the title was
offered by José González de Mendoza who said that it was selected
because it took the poet approximately that long to read the collection orally.[1] Like *6, 7 poemas, Hora y veinte* is a book of great
thematic and metric variety. It contains travel poems, love poems,
both amorous and divine, as well as cleverly contrived optical
pieces. As Luis Rius has pointed out, the book seems to be a compendium of the themes and techniques Pellicer had practiced before, but now developed with a sense of greater precision.[2] Some of
Pellicer's best attempts at optical-chromatic verse are found here.
Bearing no small trace of the vanguardisms of the 1920s with their
emphasis on unusual figures of speech, these poems attempt to
present portraits in motion.

I *"Groups of Doves"*

"Grupos de palomas" ("Groups of Doves") is a particularly telling
poem, since it appears to be the refinement of a technique which
Pellicer first experimented with in such poems as "Estudio" in *Colores en el mar*, that is, the creation of what might be called a kinetic
portrait, a picture in motion. The poem is composed of five stanzas
which evoke a series of definite visual impressions. The first stanza
creates a frame effect by first focusing on the essential visual components of the poem. Much like the optical perception of a painting
from this distance, what emerges is a generalized impression of
color and form. There is a definite synesthetic quality to the opening
lines where a group of doves are first linked to the notes of the
musical scale and then compared to the strokes of color of a painter's

77

brush. This attempt to relate several artistic mediums, to point to the harmony of different or opposing impulses produced by a work of art, is a signal characteristic of Pellicer's work:[3]

> Groups of doves,
> Notes, clefs, rests, changes of tempo,
> Vary the rhythm of the hill.
> Aware of her iridescence here one preens
> The bright circlets of her neck
> As rearward she eyes her neighbor. . . .

> Los grupos de palomas,
> notas, claves, silencios, alteraciones,
> modifican el ritmo de la loma.
> La que se sabe tornasol afina
> las ruedas luminosas de su cuello
> con mirar hacia atras a su vecina. . . .
>
> (162)

In stanzas two through four, Pellicer focuses on portraits of individual birds. There is a definite shift in tone and feeling as the poet moves away from the stylized impression of the first stanza to create humorous pictures of the various birds. The last stanza relates the parts to the whole by culminating with a vertiginous picture of the doves' flight. It is important to note that here, as in several of the travel poems in *Piedra de sacrificios*, the poet plays with the normative laws of spatial perception:

> An automobile passes; away fly the doves.
> In the arithmetic of the flight
> The eight arabs separate and weave,
> And the count comes out wrong. The sky moves,
> And the house whirls around again. . . .

> Corre un automóvil y las palomas vuelan.
> En la aritmética del vuelo,
> los ocho árabes desdóblanse
> y la suma es impar. Se mueve el cielo
> y la casa se vuelve redonda. . . .
>
> (163)

Andrew Debicki has perceptively noted that Pellicer has transformed an ordinary scene into a poetic *tour de force* through the use

of multiple perspectives. Debicki notes that throughout the poem
the doves have become a medium through which the poet focuses
on the multiplicity of possibilities within a single scene. He wrote:
"Had this poem limited itself to one of its perspectives, it would
have remained a rather good example of conventional metaphor. By
combining and counterposing them all, it becomes a dramatic embodiment of the power of poetry. The theme of artistic expression is
of course introduced directly in the first stanza. But the value of
poetry and the arts becomes much more meaningful to us as we
observe all the different visions which the poet Pellicer here weaves
out of his ordinary scene. (The whimsical ending, making us notice
the presence of a speaker-poet who has been remaking reality in this
work, underlines this subject one more time.)"[4]

II *"Study"*

Many of the same techniques (enumeration, personification) are
apparent in his second poem entitled "Estudio" ("Study"), a
twenty-eight-line poem dedicated to Mexican composer Carlos
Chávez (1899–). The piece is basically a description of an animated
still life, the portrait of a bowl of fruit which takes on anthropomorphic qualities. The poet constructs this portrait poem by a gradual
accretion of independent visual images: a hastily painted water-
melon which witnesses the rising of dawn, pineapples which salute
the moon, etc. Beginning with line 13, the poet shifts from a third-
person description of the individual pieces of fruit to first-person
narration with a one-line exclamation. Thus the line between inanimate and animate further blurs when the poet refers to "proud"
guanábanes and chicozapotes "covered with woman's things." The
last four lines create a frame effect for the entire poem, linking the
individual images:

> From an obsidian knife-blade
> the sun laughed at the display of fruits,
> and the open window let in the mountains
> slowly journeying their accustomed routes.[5]

> Desde un cuchillo de obsidiana
> reía el sol la escena de las frutas.
> Y la ventana abierta hacía entrar la montaña
> con los pequeños viajes de sus rutas.

(168)

Perhaps there is an element of parody in "Estudio," since at first blush it calls to mind the efforts of the modernists to signal a correspondence between various artistic mediums and, in particular, to reproduce as exactly as possible the details of a painting. While the poem does evoke a series of definite visual impressions, they are not ones which call to mind a single painting but rather an entire spectrum of feelings and senses related to painting as an artistic medium.

A further example of Pellicer's manipulation of color and perspective is the seven-part "Semana holandesa" ("Dutch week") a group of visual impressions of Holland which are each entitled with a day of the week. The language here, particularly the emphasis on unusual juxtaposition, is more clearly learned than felt and represents one of Pellicer's boldest excursions into the world of vanguardism. The only unifying element in the group is the poet's repeated references to painting and painters. For example, in the first poem Pellicer directly salutes his "beloved colors," while in the second there appears a reference to Rembrandt and in the fourth to Jan Vermeer.

In the "Dutch Week" sequence Pellicer culminated a number of the techniques which he had employed in embryonic form several years earlier. The first and most apparent is the painting motif, that is, the relationship between poetry and the plastic arts. In the selection entitled "Viernes" ("Friday") the poet-narrator calls attention to this relationship by directly addressing the colors of the painter's palette:

> Well, precious colors, I greet you.
> And this shirt-sleeved landscape
> who no one cares about but me
> is testimony only to cows and fluttering handkerchiefs.

> Y bien, queridos colores, os saludo.
> Y este paisaje en mangas de camisa
> que no le importa a nadie más que a mí
> es sólo fe de vacas y pañuelos de brisa.
>
> (179)

In the next stanza there is a deliberate attempt to evoke sensations of internal motion, depth, and perspective. Pellicer speaks of windmills which "think about aviation" and bikes with "heads and hearts." All, he ironically adds, live in a clean "absence of poets." Another feature of these poems is the almost exclusive use of the first-person perspective. Pellicer stresses constantly that the reality he is describing is a highly personal interpretation of the world and as such is more of a creation than a reproduction. For example, in "Domingo" ("Sunday") a Sunday banquet is transformed into a gallery of unusual impressions. The dinner table becomes a "monument to heroes," a fish, "a medieval knight," and the tropical fruits "badges to be worn at tropical garden parties."

The tongue-in-cheek cleverness and verbal gymnastics of these poems are nicely balanced by a series of more muted love poems. As we have seen, amatory and, above all, confessional verse, is a rarity with Pellicer. Nonetheless, there is an echo of vanguardist poetic diction in "Paisaje" ("Landscape"), where the poet declares:

> And while I prayed with my mother . . .
> I still saw the blind add,
> divide and multiply stars. . . .
>
> Y mientras rezaba con mi madre . . .
> aun yo veía a los ciegos sumar,
> dividir y multiplicar las estrellas . . .

> (166)

Poems in praise of Christ are also in evidence in *Hora y veinte*. Both the initial and final verses of the book, "Variaciones sobre un tema de viaje" ("Variations on a Travel Theme") and "Ruego" ("I Beseech"), praise the Divine. In the first, a rambling compendium of travel experiences, Pellicer devotes some twenty-seven stanzas to the recollection of his stay in Palestine—an event which is described as a complete religious experience. "Ruego," more lyric and elegiac than "Variaciones," is an entreaty to Christ to purify the poet.

III *Landscape Poems*

"El recuerdo" ("The Memory") is among the finest examples of Pellicer's ability to link emotion with landscape. The poem is an extended meditation on the omnipresence of the Creator, an evocation of one of those tranquil moments in life when time seems momentarily suspended and man is able to briefly feel the presence of the Divine:

In the hours
When the landscape empties,
(Clouds have borne everything away)
—Familiar objects,
Intimate words.
In a solitude of all things
Blind, mute, I have but a few fingers left
To feel the stones and roses
You touched.)

En las horas
en que el paisaje se vacía
—todo se lo han llevado las nubes—,
los objetos de familia,
las palabras íntimas.
En una soledad de todas las cosas,
ciego, mudo, sólo me quedan unos cuantos dedos
para tocar las piedras y las rosas
que tú tocaste.

                                                                    (161)

What is unique about the poem is that an almost totally emotional, abstract experience is presented as a phenomenon which is perceptible by the senses of touch and smell, for here Pellicer speaks of hands which "see" and "hear."

Along with his poem in praise of the Creator, Pellicer also included a long "Elegía Ditirámbica" ("Dithyrambic Elegy" [169–72]), which he dedicated to Simón Bolívar. This poem represents a repeated tendency in Pellicer to mingle classical metric structure with his own tropical, indigenous, poetic diction. It can be roughly divided into three parts: (1) a description of a funeral cortege carrying Bolívar's body; (2) a brief narration of the liberator's life and deeds; and (3) a return to the portrayal of the cortege with an emphasis on failure of Bolívar's ideals. Although the poem is obviously inspired in the form of the traditional elegy, it incorporates many characteristics unique to Pellicer. One of its interesting structural aspects is the rhythmic alternation between third-person objective description and first-person epic narration. While the poem begins with a portrait of Bolívar's cortege cast in brilliant visual images, beginning with line 20 there is a sudden shift to the first person. This sudden shift in focus begins a process of gradual emotional and dramatic buildup which is clearly directed from the perspective of the narrator. What begins as a highly personal lament is soon transformed and universalized into a dirge for Simón Bolívar—mythic hero. With line 30 the persona assumes the posture of a poet-seer when he declares:

> I was born to sing in the plazas
> of cities and towns
> about the magic life of that man.
>
> He nacido para cantar en las plazas
> de ciudades y pueblos
> la vida mágica de aquel hombre.

(170)

The insertion of these lines at this point in the poem is a key to understanding its success in aesthetic terms, for what Pellicer has done is to imbue the narrator with a sense of epic verisimilitude. What follows is the steady metamorphosis of Bolívar into a mythic hero through an interweaving of Christian and pre-Columbian religious symbols. For example, Bolívar's death is directly compared to that of the important Nahuatl deity Quetzalcóatl (lines 76–78). On a metaphoric level, too, there is a blending of rather traditional poetic conceits with Pellicer's recurrent anthropomorphic nature images of sun, rain, and thunder.

Apart from the amatory and hero worship poems, the most generalized impression left by the remaining selections is a trace of vague melancholy and longing for his equatorial homeland, an area which seems to exert an almost geotropic pull on the poet. Many of these poems were written after a considerable absence from Mexico. The poet's homesickness is most apparent in "Oda al sol de París" ("Ode to the Parisian Sun") and "París, canción de primavera" ("Paris, Song of Spring"). Although stylistically it is not an innovative piece, "Canción de primavera" is an effective evocation of Pellicer's pervasive yearning to return to the tropics. The poem is built around a series of contrasting impressions of the tropics and a Parisian spring. The poet exclaims: "There's something of Xochimilco/ in the sad Parisian plazas" ("Hay algo de Xochimilco/ en las plazas tristes de París" [189]). Again echoing José Vasconcelos' theory of tropical origins, Pellicer universalizes his experience in lines 33–39 by comparing his feelings to those of equatorial man in general. A vaguely reminiscent identification between meridional cultures is

also drawn in "En Atenas" ("In Athens") where a view of the ancient
Greek city acts as a catalyst for the poet's creative powers. It is as if
Greek and pre-Hispanic civilizations were linked through a subcon-
scious or archetypal level of thought.

Pellicer's most significant statement about tropical life is found in
a grouping of four poems entitled "Estudios" ("Studies"). In almost
Proustian fashion, the poet plays with the concept of time as he had
before with geometrical shapes and colors. The first three poems are
identified by Roman numerals and serve as a backdrop and introduction for the longer, culminating poem, "No hay tiempo para el
tiempo" ("There's no Time for Time"). In stanzas 1 and 3, Pellicer
suggests through paradoxic statement and a collage of time images
that the passage of time is not necessarily a measurable period during which an action or condition exists or continues but rather, in
terms reminiscent of the poet-critic Octavio Paz, he alludes to a
unique, rhythmic, poetic, tropical time:

> The hours become thin;
> out of one come ten.
> This is the tropics,
> marvelous and sad.
> Nobody knows what time it is.

> Las horas se adelgazan;
> de una salen diez.
> Es el trópico,
> prodigioso y funesto.
> Nadie sabe qué hora es.

>   (191)

The three prefatory selections climax in a dazzling portrait of
sensuous tropical beauty, beauty which more than a transcription of
visual nature images, emerges as an embodiment of tropical
timelessness. Lines 1–22 appear to echo the feeling of the first three
poems as flora and fauna become symbols of tropical essence. The
abstract is temporarily concretized. Pellicer describes a voluptuous,
almost palpable world of dazzling oases, nakedness, sensual waters,
of giant cedar and ceiba trees, a world permeated by a feeling of
sadness, a world where clocks lose time and where herons hold time
motionless:

> Sleep.—Nakedness.—Sensual waters.
> The ceiba trees become stylized.
> Three thousand cedars are born. . . .
> Sadness;
> always great, noble, and new.
> Clocks lose time;
> idleness is perfected. . . .

> Sueño. Desnudez. Aguas sensuales.
> Las ceibas se estilizan. Nacen tres mil cedros. . . .
> Tristeza.
> Siempre grande, noble y nueva.
> Los relojes se atrasan,
> se perfecciona la pereza. . . .

(192)

The mythic underpinnings of the poem become more apparent when in lines 22–29 there is a direct reference to the deity Quetzal-coatl, who appears as a mysterious symbol of cyclical time. These lines, which briefly depict his appearance and disappearance, take on greater meaning when it is recalled that in addition to his role as Wind God and creator of the universe, Quetzalcoatl incarnated the death-rebirth cycle. For example, the *Annals of Cuauhtitlan* state that: ". . . they say that when Quetzalcoatl died he was not seen for four days, because then he went to dwell among the dead; and that also in four days he was furnished with arrows; so that in eight days there appeared the great star called Quetzalcoatl."[6] The implicit reference to cyclical or mythic time made in the representation of Quetzalcoatl becomes explicit in the final stanza where "slow, fecund, lazy" tropical time is born again.

With the publication of *Hora y veinte*, Pellicer entered the world of those young poets recognized in international Hispanic circles. Writing in *El Mercurio* from Santiago, Chile, Gabriela Mistral dubbed him "Un poeta nuevo de América" ("a new American poet") and two reviews of his works were published in the important Mexican journals, *Revista de Revistas (Review of Reviews)* and *Contemporáneos (Contemporaries)*. In the former journal, the critic J. M. González de Mendoza commented on the personal circumstances which gave rise to the publication of *Hora y veinte* and noted Pellicer's affinity for tactile imagery: "For Carlos Pellicer, like

Théophile Gautier, the exterior world exists. He needs to see, to hear, to smell, to taste, to touch. He has achieved his most brilliant successes when he has transcribed in his poems the clever relations that his aquiline eye perceives between things."[7] Ortiz de Monte-llano's review, "Un camino de poesía" ("A Road of Poetry"), published in *Contemporáneos*, made some even more penetrating observations on Pellicer's verse. After making the customary comments on the plasticity of his language, the critic notes that the poet's attitude toward nature approaches that of a pantheist: "the pantheism of Pellicer's poetry is civilized, sportive, without interior drama, a poetry of beautiful plastic tones."[8] Montellano then underscored the thematic duality of the poet: "Epic raptures, Greek accents, and Quetzal plumes are mixed with dove nests in this primitive and modern artistic world."[9] The opposing terms, primitive and modern, are descriptive of two forces operative in Pellicer's poetry: a linguistic and philosophic debt to pre-Columbian mythology juxtaposed with an interest in contemporary imagistic verse. This dualism is fundamental to the appreciation of Pellicer's poetic art.

CHAPTER 6

Highway: *The Plateau*

I *Memories of Things Past*

PELLICER'S fifth book of verse, *Camino (Highway)*, a collection of fifteen poems, was published in Paris in 1929. It is a potpourri of many different types of poems which reflect his experiences as a traveler to the Middle East, the Mediterranean, and Northern Europe. As in the case of his other books, it is difficult to isolate a specific link which unifies all the poems. It is best to think of the book as a loosely connected group of associated poems. The scope of theme is broad, ranging from a melancholy evocation of a past love affair in the eight-sonnet group entitled "Elegía" ("Elegy"), to brilliant color portraits of exotic cities in such poems as "Brujas" ("Brugge"), "El mar Jónico" ("The Ionian Sea"), "Estrofa neoyorquina" ("Strophe to New York"), and "Estudios venecianos" ("Studies of Venice") as well as religious poems such as "La hora de David" ("David's Hour"). From a stylistic point of view, however, *Camino* is a book which seems to mark a plateau in his evolution. In fact, many of the selections immediately call to mind the poet's earliest experiments with pictorial verse. A third poem entitled "Estudio" ("Study"), consisting of eleven synesthetic impressions of the Syrian landscape, could well have appeared in *Colores en el mar*. It is an exact parallel to "Recuerdos de Iza" ("Memories of Iza"), inasmuch as the poem consists of a series of independent verse-strophes which collectively evoke a multisensory impression of the Syrian landscape. As in the Japanese haiku there is an effort to capture the essence of the poetic moment through the suppression of the anecdotal and superfluous:

> 1) The blue Syrian towns
>   Where there are only glances and smiles.

4) There is an orange thirst
   next to the afternoon still high.

5) The water in the jugs
   tastes of birds.

1) Los pueblos azules de Siria
   donde no hay más que miradas y sonrisas.

4) Hay una sed de naranja
   junto a la tarde todavía muy alta.

5) El agua de los cántaros
   sabe a pájaros.

                                                        (218)

In addition to the purely descriptive works in *Camino*, Pellicer included a number of poems in which he again returned to the theme of poetry. In fact, the book begins with a poem entitled "A la poesía" ("To Poetry") in which Pellicer personifies verse by comparing the creative act to the sowing and reaping of a field of wheat. In many ways the poem is reminiscent of "El segador" ("The Sower") and "El sembrador" ("The Reaper") which appeared in 6, 7 *poemas*. The poem begins with an elusive reference to the mysterious relationships between poetry and poet. Beginning with stanzas four through eight Pellicer develops the central metaphor of the poem: the creative act is directly compared to the reaping of the autumn harvest. Merlin Forster put it this way: "The poet gathers with the brilliant sickle of his intuition the golden grains of the nutritive and cosmic poetic wheat."[1]

In the midst of the ears of wheat
and under your summerly gaze
I sharpened the sickle which joins the starry harvest
to the day.

En medio de las espigas
y a tu mirada estival,
afilé la hoz que alía al día
la cosecha sideral.

                                                        (205)

A much more ethereal depiction of poetry appears in "El encuentro" ("The Encounter"). Here poetry is depicted as a mysterious force which eludes description, a seductive temptress who calls to him from the dark of the night:

> From whence do you come? You, whose glances
> fill me with new sensations.
> You rise up in the midst of my life
> like a cypress next to a star.

> ¿De dónde vienes tú cuyas miradas
> crearon para mí nuevos sentidos?
> y tú surges en medio de mi vida
> semejante a un ciprés junto a una estrella.

(248)

"Fragmentos" ("Fragments") personifies not poetry but its component parts—words, "the childish throng." The poem is divided into five stanzas each labeled with a letter of the alphabet. In the first stanza, Pellicer playfully addresses words, the poet's tools, which he organizes to recount the beauties of his beloved. Her image is evoked through the blending of several sensory responses—auditory, olfactory, tactile, and visual:

> As if you had just cut an apple
> your hands were agile, aromatic.
> Your voice had the touch of amber lights,
> etched out against a sky of hope.

> Cual si vinieses de cortar una manzana
> tus manos eran ágiles y aromas.
> Tu voz tenía el tacto de las luces del ámbar,
> de perfil sobre un cielo de esperanza.

(221)

II   *"Elemental Poem"*

There are scattered references to poetry in other poems, but the most striking allusion to the act of poetic creation appears in the six-part "Poema elemental" ("Elemental Poem"). It is a description

of the four primordial elements of life: air, fire, water, and earth.[2] In
a style reminiscent of works such as "Uxmal," Pellicer maintains an
objective distance from the reader, evoking a complex portrait of
cosmic harmony and subtle natural interrelationships. The poem is
at once both an explicit description of the visual splendors of the
physical world and an implicit metaphor of creation, both cosmic
and poetic.

The basic conceptual matrix of "Poema elemental"—the theory of
the four elements—has been fused with yet another mythic sub-
strata relating to pre-Hispanic thought. In Western thought the
theory that the earth is comprised of four elements can be traced to
the fifth century B.C. Greek philosopher Empedocles who divided
all matter into four essential components: fire, air, water, and earth.
The literary use of the motif became stylized during the Renaissance
through a complex system of metaphors which reflected a concept of
the universe as a state of balance and harmony between opposing
natural elements.[3]

The initial four strophes are dedicated to a description of the
elements, stressing their essentially tactile qualities. In the first
stanza, "Aire" ("Air"), Pellicer stresses transparency and trans-
lucence—the characteristic of air—by metaphorically relating these
optical qualities to other sense perceptions. Air becomes both a
"rose" and a "transparent fruit." In the second, "El agua" ("Water"),
moisture is depicted as "palpating space." Here a blend of biblical
and mythological allusions evoke a feeling of timelessness and eternal recurrence. The poet refers to "the regal waters of a fantastic
journey" ("Aguas reales del viaje fabuloso" [208]) and recalls how "a
drop of water/ . . . made Susana's body tremble/ amid the biblical
chaff of the bath" ("una gota de agua/ . . . hizo temblar el dorso de
Susana/ entre las barbas bíblicas del baño" [208]).

"El fuego" ("Fire") emerges in the third stanza through a series of
anthropomorphic images: "on finger tips/ the night is held up/ aerial
and enormous" ("Sobre la yema de los dedos/ se sostiene la noche/
aérea y enorme" [208]). The sun is next depicted as the central
ordering element in cosmic harmony: "The soul rests in the center/
of the vast astronomical landscape" ("El espíritu reposa en el seno/
del vasto paisaje astronómico" [208]). Through a linking of thermal
and water images, the sun's rays are next related to the sea. The
poet develops an awesome awareness of cosmic unity by the image
of an enormous, encircling sphere of fire in which the sea and air are

joined metaphorically. It is as if the earth is viewed from a great distance, a remote vantage point from which the poet discerns man's creations.

"La Tierra" ("The Earth") concludes the enumeration; but here the tone of mythic awe has been replaced by an attitude of earthy joy, a warm response to the creative potential of the natural world. The poet refers to the smells of the land and sea. Earth is viewed as a woman wooed by the other elements. Their fusion is depicted as a fertile union:

> The happy land, as beautiful as the cursed land.
> The sea which woos her
> and the air which sees her naked,
> join their triple brows when ancient dawn
> unites in a fertile act land and fire. . . .

> La tierra feliz, tan bella como la tierra maldita.
> El mar que la enamora
> y el aire que la ve desnuda,
> juntan las cejas triples cuando la antigua aurora
> une en acto fecundo tierra y fuego
>
> (209)

After addressing death, which gives a cyclical quality to the poem, Pellicer appends a dedication to poetry—the force which has given life to these abstractions.

> In the beginning, the enriched hand
> with water cut the diamond and hurled at the fire
> of the poem, the forces of life.

> Elemental, la mano enriquecida
> rayó el agua al diamante y echó al fuego
> del poema, las fuerzas de la vida.
>
> (210)

"Poema elemental" may be examined from several perspectives. At first one notices the structural symmetry of the composition and is reminded of its similarity with the seventeenth-century poem by Calderón de la Barca addressed to these same elements. Like Calderón, Pellicer has employed the Renaissance technique of dissemination and recapitulation, closing the poem with a synthetic summary stanza where the elements reappear linked in a state of balanced harmony, since the element of poetry seems to serve here as a catalyst. On the other hand, and bearing in mind the recurrent appearance of pre-Columbian motifs in Pellicer's verse, it may be possible to study "Poema elemental" from the point of view of Nahuatl symbolic language. It will be recalled that the nucleus of the poem is composed of five stanzas, with the sixth, labeled "Envío" ("Shipment"), appended as a summary. Not only myths but all the symbolic manifestations of Nahuatl (Aztec) culture are permeated, as Laurette Séjourné has deduced, by the idea of four primordial elements redeemed by a unifying center. Séjourné later quotes Alfonso Caso, who likewise emphasized that "this fundamental idea of four cardinal points and a central area . . . which forms the fifth or central area, is found in all the religious expressions of the Aztec people."[4] Thus, while the first four stanzas of the poem describe in turn, the attributes of air, water, fire, and land, the fifth stanza, "La muerte" ("Death"), is presented as a unifying central force:

> Much like God's shadow
> which watches land and fire, air and sea
> it brings an order which diminishes and augments
> the remainder and the sum total.

> Semejante a la sombra de Dios
> que vigila la tierra y el fuego y el aire y el mar,
> trae el orden que disminuye y aumenta,
> la resta y la suma total.
>
> (210)

Why this fifth or central stanza bears the name of death may be further clarified by noting that the central deity in Nahuatl-Aztec religion, Quetzalcoatl, the God of life and image of creative duality, was often linked with the death-resurrection cycle, as we have seen in "Estudio" from *Hora y veinte*. As Séjourné writes, "If we remember that Quetzalcoatl left his kingdom only after an experience that has all the appearance of a death through initiation—four days enclosed in a stone coffin—we may suppose that the neophyte took the road of Miccaotli only after symbolically abandoning his earthly swaddling clothes."[5] There is a second point which merits attention. Nahuatl cosmology is ruled by another tenet which is a corollary of the first—the vital impulse which arises from the union of opposing elements. The Aztecs thought creative energy sprang from a fusion of nature's forces. This idea is illustrated in the fourth stanza, "La Tierra" ("The Earth"), where the elements join in a fertile union.

It is appropriate to make a parenthetical observation here concerning the concept of the quincunx (a five point figure) just discussed and its possible relationship to the poetic diction of Pellicer. The concise quincunx symbolized the union of four opposing forces at the center. The "Law of the Center" is consequently the regulatory principle in the whole of Nahuatl-Aztec symbolism, since it was at the center of the universe where the creative union between matter and spirit was to take place. Because, as Séjourné notes, "the supreme reality lives at the very center of matter, the variety of forms assumed by Nature in her animal and vegetable kingdoms are considered . . . outer manifestations of this reality."[6] This gave rise, the critic points out, to a dazzling series of images. We have already noted repeatedly in Pellicer's poetry an emphasis on nature imagery—vegetable, animal, celestial—which bears resemblance to such pre-Columbian prototypes. In short, Pellicer's "Poema elemental," a dazzling ode to the life forces of nature, is a work which clearly points to a confluence of two traditions in his poetry—the pre-Columbian and the Hispanic.

In summary, it could be said that while the compositions in *Camino* are longer, more polished and technically balanced than those in previous books, it never achieved critical popularity. It was as if the poet had reached a plateau with these highly polished descriptive poems slowly elaborated from much shorter imagistic verses in *Colores en el mar* and gradually expanded into more complex, vaguely rhetorical pieces. While there are individual poems of considerable merit in this book, collectively speaking it is not an impressive collection, and certainly if Pellicer had continued to work the same travel poem motif, his career would not have achieved the dimensions it did.

CHAPTER 7

On the Road to Maturity

I Hymn to the Tropics

IN 1937, after a lapse of some eight years, Pellicer published a group of twenty-four poems under the title *Hora de junio* (*Hour of June*), a book which firmly cemented his reputation as poet. As he had done with earlier collections, Pellicer began *Hora de junio* with a short epigraph in verse which set the tone for the collection. Echoing his earlier quest for substantiality, he indicates here that he is surfeited with artificial beauty and wants to achieve a more transcendent aesthetic experience:

Hour of June

> Still green grain, April's life-force
> Just one thrust of the oar to reach
> the edge of the high sea!
> The graceful body yearns not for beauty alone,
> but infinity. Oh, nameless beauty,
> Oh, infinity!

> Espiga verde aún, fuerza de abril, ligera.
> ¡Ya de un golpe de remo y a la orilla
> de alta mar!
> El cuerpo hermoso quiere el infinito
> y ya no la belleza. ¡La belleza
> sin nombre, oh infinito!

(255)

The book opens with the thirteen-stanza "Esquemas para una oda tropical" ("Sketches for a Tropical Ode") which was dedicated to the Mexican poet Jorge Cuesta (1903–1942) and had been published as a pamphlet by the Mexican Ministry of Foreign Relations in 1933.[1] It is one of Pellicer's most technically complex and important poems. Pellicer has referred to it modestly as one of his "least defective poems."[2] It is a work which exemplifies Pellicer's masterful sense of balance and form. Here the poet restates in more specific language the quincunx motif first alluded to in "Poema elemental." This hymn to the tropics takes the form of a ritualistic incantation couched in pre-Hispanic symbolic language. The poem builds dramatically from a two-stanza introduction which hints at the impending arrival of the voice of the tropics from the four cardinal points of the globe and the culminating center of the poet's own existence:

> The four-voiced tropical ode
> should arrive seated in a great swing
> of orchid-garland ropes.
>
> From the south it will come, from the east and the west,
> from the winged north; from the culminating center
> of my life's truncated pyramid.[3]
>
> La oda tropical a cuatro voces
> ha de llegar sentada en la mecida
> que amarró la guirnalda de la orquídea.
>
> Vendrá del Sur, del Este y del Oeste,
> del Norte avión, del Centro que culmina
> la pirámide trunca de mi vida.

(256)

The third stanza signals an important change in point of view. With the introduction of a cluster of images suggestive of a ritual initiation, the persona is transformed into a poet-seer. Thus Pellicer radically alters the relationship between the poem and the reader by shifting the narrative base to a level of fantasy and magic. The poem ceases to be a description and becomes an intensely personal vision of the tropics.

> I want my feet burned in braziers
> of the loneliest anguish;
> I want to go out naked toward the poem,
> the poem with airy sandals
> other innocent pores give it.

> Yo quiero arder mis pies en los braseros
> de la angustia más sola,
> para salir desnudo hacia el poema
> con las sandalias de aire que otros poros
> inocentes le den.
>
> (256)

Stanzas four and five subtly allude to the dawning of a tropical day. In the sixth stanza the image of the poet-seer emerges again with an allusion to poetry as catalytic force. The image of the pyramid and the implicit reference to the "Law of the Center" in the second stanza is now heightened by a further allusion to the same motif:

> So my voice in the center of the four
> fundamental voices
> will bear on its shoulders
> the weight of birds of paradise.

> Así mi voz al centro de las cuatro
> voces fundamentales
> tendría sobre sus hombros
> el peso de las aves del paraíso.
>
> (257)

Stanzas seven through nine become more abstract and visual as the poet attempts to portray sensuously the essence of tropical life. It is a world permeated by the faint smell of custard-apple, cooled by the dark quietness of thick forests, filtered by lemon-tree breezes and dominated by the ancient iguana—symbol of eternal recurrence who "was, is, and will be." The first-person narrator again emerges in the tenth stanza where Pellicer recounts a fleeting hallucination he experienced while bathing in an underground pool in Chichén-Itzá. This puzzling anecdote, perhaps an allusion to a vision of Quetzalcoatl, is followed in the eleventh stanza by a description of jungle foliage dependent on the nutritive powers of the tropical sun for its existence. In the twelfth stanza the motif of the four elements appears again as a symbolic representation of natural harmony:

> The profound tropics
> sustain in living flesh the beauty
> of creation. Earth, water, air, fire,
> to the south, north, east, and west
> concenter the essential seeds,

the sky of surprises,
the pure nakedness of the hours,
and the sound of the vast solitudes.

El trópico entrañable
sostiene en carne viva la belleza
de Dios. La tierra, el agua, el aire, el fuego,
al Sur, al Norte, al Este, y al Oeste
concentran las semillas esenciales
el cielo de sorpresas
la desnudez intacta de las horas
y el ruido de las vastas soledades.

(258)

The poem culminates with a projection of the arrival of the tropic ode—the force of poetry—which is depicted through a dazzling portrait of multiple transfigurations in which the persona envisions himself invaded by the forces of poetry and at the same time metamorphosized into various animal and vegetable forms. The two levels of the poem, the hallucinatory voice of the persona and the sensuous world of animal and vegetable images, fuse in this final moment when the narrator transcends the physical and temporal limitations of this world to become one with nature.

The tropical ode in four voices
will come, word for word,
to drink at my lips, . . .
and disseminate me in itself
so that I shall be through words,
palms and antelope,
ceiba and alligator, fern and lyrebird,
tarantula and orchid, mocking bird and anaconda.
Then I shall be a cry, a lone clear cry.

La oda tropical a cuatro voces
podrá llegar, palabra por palabra,
a beber en mis labios, . . .
y a esparcirme en sí misma,
a que yo sea a vuelta de palabras,
palmera y antílope,
ceiba y caimán, helecho y ave-lira,
tarántula y orquídea, zenzontle y anaconda.
Entonces seré un grito, un solo grito claro.

(259)

The climax of the poem is perfectly in accord with its dramatic structure, since as early as the third stanza the poet had signaled that he was operating on a magical or intuitive level of reality. In addition, the transfiguration images of the closing lines are clearly related to the mythic underpinnings of the poem if it is recalled that the process of transfiguration was integrally related to a number of pre-Columbian religious beliefs.

The motif of the four elements appears again in the five-part poem "La voz" ("The Voice"). Here Pellicer clearly evinces his pantheistic world view when he compares the act of poetic creation to the act of cosmic creation. The first poem in the series describes the creation of the world as a ritual fertility act. The poet states that when the world was created the earth and the elements of which it is composed were infused with the voices of creation. He now seeks to become one with this creative whole. In the final poem, Pellicer hints that man can only find union with nature through a concentrated awareness of experience in language, through poetry.

In addition to the initial "Esquemas para una oda tropical," many of the poems in *Hora de junio* are pictorial celebrations of tropical life. As we have seen in his earlier poems, Pellicer has a special fascination for landscape poetry. His landscapes and seascapes are deceptive, for they are not in the traditional sense of the word descriptions of the natural world, but highly personal re-creations of a scene or moment. There are at least four important landscape poems in *Hora de junio:* "Poética del paisaje" ("Landscape poetics"), "Retórica del paisaje" ("Rhetoric of the Landscape"), "Invitación al paisaje" ("Invitation to the Landscape"), and "Poema pródigo" ("Prodigal poem"). In "Poética del paisaje" Pellicer evokes a picture of natural scenery in which the eye of the poet-narrator perceives unique spatial and chromatic affinities between the objects represented. The poem is structured around the visual impressions the poet perceives and is narrated from the perspective of the moment of creation. Personification is the dominant technique in this poem in which horizons, mountains, clouds, and birds are endowed with human characteristics.

"Retórica del paisaje" describes the landscape from an aerial perspective and calls to mind the "Suite brasilera: poemas aéreos" from *Piedra de sacrificios*. In the third stanza, Pellicer makes an important observation concerning the poet's relationship to reality by stressing the essentially Creationist stance of the author:

> Because reality is a thing of my own,
> that is to say, something you will never see,
> as the proffered eyes
> upon a plate of Santa Lucía
> (Courtesy of Roman Church which you are prone to
> reject.)[4]

> Porque la realidad es cosa mía,
> es decir, lo que usted nunca verá,
> en un plato le da Santa Lucía
> los ojos convenientes. (Cortesía
> de la Iglesia Romana que usted devolverá.)

(282)

Pellicer's dual tendency to personify both nature and poetry is brilliantly synthesized in "Invitación al paisaje." Similar to many of his landscape poems, it is an apostrophe to nature. The poet's desire to personify and concretize the abstract is immediately apparent. In contrast to many of the landscape poems in *Hora de junio* which might be described as vaguely diffuse and rhetorical, "Invitación al paisaje" is constructed around a rather clearly perceptible plan. The twelve-stanza poem consists of an accretion of images related to various natural phenomena (rivers, mountains, clouds, shadows) which are presented as if they were perceived through the intuitive powers of the poet rather than merely through the senses. In the final stanza these multiple impressions are linked in a single visual image where the most abstract and intuitive of the mental processes, the creative act, is presented as a physical, tactile phenomenon. The entire poem may be thought of as an extended metaphor of poetic creation.

II Hours of June

Unlike the majority of Pellicer's collections of poetry which have no real unity of theme, *Hora de junio* is held together by a series of love sonnets all entitled "Horas de junio" which describe an unhappy love affair. They are dispersed throughout the book alternating with the more visually concrete and less philosophical landscape poems. Although collectively the poems tell a story of unrequited love, they do so indirectly. The first grouping is composed of three separate sonnets brought together under the heading "Horas de junio." In the first poem, Pellicer sets a tone of melancholy and introspection by complaining of a lack of poetic inspiration. The next two poems narrate the story of an unfulfilled love affair which took place one year before. Pellicer translates this emotional abstraction into a tactile, sensory experience.

The next grouping consists of two sonnets linked to the poems already discussed by the reappearance of an important water image and the concomitant stress on poetic impotence. This love-poetry motif appears again in a third two-sonnet series where Pellicer introduces the theme of artistic doubt. Carolyn Schalck has explicated this poem in the following manner: "The two tercets describe the poet's quest of the ultimate poetic excellence, symbolized by a rose. In order to reach this flower, the poet must prick his fingers on the thorns and bleed. Even when after much suffering he reaches the bloom, he realizes that it has changed into another flower which is itself not determined. In other words, poetry cannot be defined."[5]

In the fourth and fifth sonnet groupings, Pellicer leaves the question of the love-poetry relationship and focuses on the cosmic aspect of his love affair. Thus, in the fourth poem, he equates the union of man and woman to the blossoming of an aquatic plant.

The grouping of poems entitled "Horas de junio" illustrates with particular clarity the primitive-modern dichotomy noted in Pellicer's poetry. While in their external sonnet form and general melancholy tone, the poems may be classified as traditional or conventional, there is a constant leitmotiv of suggestive vegetable and animal imagery running through these poems which together with metaphoric references to the concept of creative union, call to mind Pellicer's important debt to pre-Columbian ritual and myth.

III   Hexagons

While in general terms the verse of *Hora de junio* might be called restrained or meditative, the publication of *Exágonos (Hexagons)* in 1941 marks an abrupt return to the imagistic poetry of Pellicer's youth. Dedicated to the poet José Juan Tablada, the book is composed of twenty-one six-line poems written in free verse together with one ten-line poem. There is no thematic unity in this collection and little seriousness of purpose. With limited exceptions, such as a brief poem to Simón Bolívar, the remaining lines are playful in tone and deliberately contrived in structure:

> Where is my heart going
> along this luminous avenue?

Good night, Doña Disillusion.
Yes, I was in the provinces
Mortgaging sunsets
in order to build my life!

¿A dónde va mi corazón
por esta luminosa avenida?
Buenas noches, doña desilusión.
¡Si yo estaba por la provincia
hipotecando puestas de sol
para edificar mi vida!

(316)

A review which appeared in the *Handbook of Latin American Studies* typifies the negative critical reaction to the book: "A score of six-line poems (hence the name, although the usual spelling is 'hexágono'), with no definite pattern; a mixture of the elegiac and the witty, often effete and trite. This minor work (verses written on board ship) reveals fundamental weaknesses which Pellicer, a poet of repute, seems to have succeeded in covering up in his more ambitious undertakings."[6] However, Lloyd Mallen, writing in the prestigious review *Poetry*, was more positive: "The third poet is Carlos Pellicer, who has often been called a painter in words. This, however, is not exactly true, for although Pellicer's images present definite pictures and colors, they do this by the subtle suggestion of his words and ideas rather than by any special imagistic emphasis on the poet's part. *Exágonos* [*Hexagons*] is a collection of six line poems, four of which have been set to music by Carlos Chávez. All of the poems were written within two days, aboard ship, as Pellicer was approaching Rio de Janeiro, a circumstance attested to by the large number of poems concerned with the sea."[7]

IV Corner and other Images

Although *Recinto y otras imágenes* (*Corner and other Images*) was published as one book in 1941, from a thematic point of view they constitute two separate works. The first, *Recinto* (*Corner*), is composed of twenty poems which describe the progress of a love affair. The title page bears the annotation "From August, 1930, to January, 1931," indicating that this was the time span during which the relationship lasted. Much as the five love sonnets in *Hora de junio* were linked by a series of recurring patterns of images, the compositions of *Recinto* have a definite thematic and stylistic symmetry. Within

the larger framework of the poems, there are two thematic sub-
groupings. Thus, the first ten poems describe the emergence and
growing intensity of Pellicer's love while the last ten depict the
falling away of the lovers and the end of the relationship. In the first
poem, Pellicer states that his attraction for his beloved is an encom-
passing experience: "And to you, for you, and in you I live and love"
("Y a ti, por ti y en ti vivo y adoro" [331]). He also establishes here
his basic metaphoric technique of identifying the beloved with the
landscape. The intensity of the mutual love relationship is so great
that in the eighth composition, the poet declares that he has become
a mere sensory echo of his lover:

> You are more than my ear because you hear
> the echo of your voice in me
> and thus I cannot hear myself because
> I'm filled with the tenderness of your accent,
> your voice alone!
>
> I am only a living mirror
> of your feelings. The fidelity
> of a lake in the crater of a volcano.

> Tú eres más que mi oído porque escuchas
> lo que en mi oído llevo de tu voz.
> Y así camino sordo de mí mismo
> lleno de las ternuras de tu acento.
> ¡La sola voz de ti!
>
> Yo solamente soy el vivo espejo
> de tus sentidos. La fidelidad
> de lago en la garganta del volcán.
>
>   (337–38)

Midway in the collection (beginning with the eleventh poem), he
announces a deterioration in their affair: "The first sadness has ar-
rived. Your eyes/ were indifferent to mine . . . ("La primera tristeza
ha llegado. Tus ojos / fueron indiferentes a los míos . . ." [340]).
Continuing with a parallel but paradoxical reverse series of nature
images, he depicts the growing coolness of his affection. While in
the first ten poems of the book the beloved was equated with lush
and viable aspects of nature—oasis, rose, mountain—she is now

described with harsh, inanimate objects—a dry stone, a pool of poison water. The somewhat caustic note of these verses gradually evolves into one of sustained melancholy, and by the last poem the poet seems reconciled to his fate and recognizes that the love has served as a source of inspiration for his muse.

In sharp contrast to the balance and symmetry of *Recinto* are the disparate compositions which compose *Otras imágenes (Other Images)*. The sixteen poems treat a wide variety of themes, ranging from descriptive travel poems to indagations into pre-Hispanic myth. Typical of Pellicer's more conventional landscape poems are the "Sonetos de otoño" ("Autumn Sonnets"). Here, as in "El segador" and "El sembrador," from *6, 7 poemas*, man and nature are fused as one life-force.

> First autumn sky, first flight
> In the blue desert of this morning.
> Sun, rise for me; and sink down distant
> Sierras where the sun melts into sky.[8]

> Primer cielo de otoño, primer vuelo
> en el desierto azul de esta mañana.
> Súbeme sol y bájame lejana
> serranía en que el sol cambia de cielo.

>   (379)

If the "Sonetos de Otoño" seem familiar in terms of diction, the "Romance de Tilantongo" ("Romance of Tilantongo") underscores the equally recurrent aspect of Pellicer's preoccupation with pre-Columbian myth. The poem was written, Pellicer has stated, on the occasion of a poetry contest which required that a poem be composed in *romance*—a ballad form written in verses of usually eight syllables—on a pre-Hispanic theme. Pellicer's source was a Mixtec legend of the Creation which he read in Burgoa's *Historia de Oaxaca (History of Oaxaca)*.

The four-part poem treats two distinct but related myths of the Creation and the founding of the region of Tilantongo. The first stanza serves as a general introduction to the entire composition. In the classical ballad tradition, the poet establishes his credentials and points out that he is an heir of the ancient Mayan culture which once flourished in Oaxaca:

I who from Tabasco come
with gods at my back,
Quetzalcoatl, Quetzalcoatl,
he of the sacred beard
he of the green cheeks. . . .

Yo que de Tabasco vengo
con dioses a las espaldas,
Quetzalcoatl, Quetzalcoatl
el de la profunda barba
el de las mejillas verdes. . . .

(349)

In the second stanza and similar to the technique used in "Ux-mal," Pellicer uses the motif of the dream experience to relate the Mixtec legend of the Creation and shifts the poem to a level of magic and fantasy. Pellicer, now the detached narrator, explains how from a glance of the gods two trees grew—one masculine, the other feminine. It was from the union of these opposing but complimentary elements that man was born: "From the love of these trees/ the human race was born in flames" (Del amor de aquellos árboles/ nació entre hogueras la raza" [352]). In the third stanza, the poet relates the myth of the founding of Tilantongo and returns in the fourth to the dream motif. The poet now awakens, closing the poem with the same lines with which it was begun.

It is difficult to perceive any appreciable thematic unity among the other poems in *Otras imágenes*. As Pellicer has admitted, a number of the selections were merely added to the collection at the urging of the publisher and have no aesthetic relationship to it as a whole. There are a number of uneven occasional poems such as "Lutos por Antonio Mercé" ("Dirge for Antonia Mercé"), "Al poeta colombiano Germán Pardo García" ("To the Colombian poet Germán Pardo García"), an "Estudio" ("Study") dedicated to Diego Rivera, and a sonnet written to commemorate the gift of a rare cactus plant to Eduardo Villaseñor. More impressive than these occasional pieces are the poems in which Pellicer deals with the theme of poetry: "A la poesía" ("To poetry") and "Estudios" ("Studies"). In the former the month of June appears as an emblem of poetic inspiration. Using a paradoxical water image, Pellicer compares the yearning for creative expression to an unquenchable thirst initiated by the warmth of a June day. The two-poem grouping, "Estudios," is a poetic query into the basis of poetry and as such calls to mind Pellicer's earlier indagations into the same theme.

CHAPTER 8

The Mature Poet: Subordinations *and* Practice of Flight

I Subordinations

IN 1949 Pellicer published a collection of twenty-six poems under the title *Subordinaciones (Subordinations)*. The book, which was dedicated to the Chilean Nobel laureate, Gabriela Mistral, was considerably more even in quality than *Recinto y otras imágenes*. Three important trends appear in *Subordinaciones:* a concern with the relationship between man and nature, a renascent interest in Hispanic hero figures, and a concomitant desire to explore the field of pre-Hispanic myth. However, it is Pellicer's Christian pantheism which critics have most noted. While some scholars have been content to label Pellicer a colorist and landscape poet *par excellence,* very little attention has been paid to the principles which govern his use of language, the internal structuring, so to speak, of his visual image clusters. Professor Frank N. Dauster was among the first to point out the inherent characteristics of Pellicer's poetry. In an important study of landscape in Pellicer's poetry, Dauster wrote: "Therefore it seems unjust to us that he continue to be labeled a landscape poet. For him poetry means the intermixture of man with nature. One of the dominant techniques in his entire work is the personification of nature."[1] Dauster's basic premise was later amplified in a doctoral dissertation by Rubén A. Gamboa who studied the poet's attitude in relation to four major themes: Americanism, nature, love, and religion. Gamboa again underscored the overriding tenet of interpenetration of man and nature. A more recent study by Francisco A. Pabón carries the argument one step further by relating Pellicer's use of nature imagery to his aesthetic world view. Pabón writes: "The poet's response to nature is expressed through a particular conception and representation of reality, which on one level is based on an indigenous poetic topology

106

. . . and on another is informed by constructivist esthetics of the twentieth century."[2]

Although we have noted a recurrent tendency in Pellicer's work to transfigure man into nature and vice versa, the technique seems to achieve its widest use in *Subordinaciones*. While in earlier collections Pellicer often compared himself with the external world, here this substructure becomes an integral part of his world view. For example, in "Discurso por las flores" ("Discourse for the Flowers"), Pellicer declares: "a bit of my consciousness . . ./ took the shape of a flower . . ." ("Algo de mi conciencia . . ./ tomó forma de flor . . ." [401]), and later, continuing the same vegetable transfiguration motif he writes:

> Something in my blood travels with a voice of chlorophyll.
> When I extend the branch of my hand to a tree
> I feel a connection. . . .
>
> Algo en mi sangre viaja con voz de clorofila.
> Cuando a un árbol le doy la rama de mi mano
> siento la conexión. . . .
>
> (401)

The significance of the poem, however, is not to be seen in a cataloging of vegetable images (although they are poetically powerful conceits), since there is a substructure of pre-Hispanic myth which integrates it as an artistic whole. Approximately halfway through the poem (stanza 8), Pellicer shifts from a personal description of his native flora to evoke the broader implications of their role in Mexican cosmology: "The Mexican peoples have had two obsessions/ A fixation with death and a love of flowers" ("El pueblo mexicano tiene dos obsesiones/ el gusto por la muerte y el amor a las flores" [402]). Through the introduction of the figures of Xochipilli, the pre-Columbian Lord of Flowers and representative of the freed spirit, who is depicted as a catalytic force in the union of opposites, Pellicer resolves the paradoxical duality of the first image and goes on later to point out the role of man in the ordering of the cosmic harmony: "And the vegetable soul that there is in human life/ creates the sky and the clouds which gild the morning" ("Y el alma vegetal que hay en la vida humana/ crea el cielo y las nubes que inventan la mañana" [403]). Man and nature again appear linked in "canto por un recuerdo Griego" ("Song for a Greek Memory").

Using the familiar framework of a travel poem, Pellicer describes the ruins of Delphi from the vantage point of the trees which surround it. While the poem is similar to several earlier descriptive travel pieces, it is a more refined product. Here Pellicer fuses his ability to evoke strong visual impressions of land and sea with his interest in the mythic substructure which links the world's ancient civilizations.

In stanzas one through three the narrator addresses his muse in a plea for total interpenetration with nature. In the following five strophes the persona stresses his Indian heritage and underscores the cultural affinities between East and West. There is a sudden shift in tone and perspective in the ninth stanza when the narrator suddenly emerges as a part of the natural world:

> And I,
> who am a
> walking mahogany tree
> Penetrated with my roots and branches
> And then ascended through the sacred rocks.

> Y yo
> que soy un árbol de caoba
> que camina,
> Penetré con raíces y ramajes
> Y después ascendí por las rocas divinas.

> (406)

What follows is a cluster of images which portray the physical, tactile aspects of the transformation as the narrator feels the sea in his lungs and senses the bombardment of a rain storm. With stanza eleven, this vision of Greek splendor vanishes as the persona is transformed physically and projected temporally into his role as a twentieth-century man. The poem closes as it began with an apostrophe to poetry. The man transformed into a tree motif appears again in "Poema en tiempo vegetal" ("Poem in Vegetable Time"), a poem in which Pellicer blends pre-Columbian myth and contemporary nationalistic pride.

II "Song of Usumacinta"

Nature imagery and pre-Columbian myth are tightly integrated in "El canto del Usumacinta" ("The Song of Usumacinta"), the most complex and subtly structured poem in the collection. Ostensibly, the poem is a hymn to the Usumacinta river which flows through Pellicer's native Tabasco. As the poet evokes the grandeur of the life-giving river, he converts it into a symbol of Mexico's subterranean but ever present pre-Columbian heritage. The men of the tropics, like the river which passes through the region, are infused, says the poet, with the past: "Those of us who were born there have our own idea/ of what the body and the soul are" ("Los que allí nacimos tenemos una idea propia/ de lo que es el alma y de lo que es el cuerpo" [473]). In a structural and thematic sense it resembles poems such as "Uxmal" and "Poema elemental" where the narrator takes the posture of the inspired, all-seeing poet-seer, who recounts a myth from the detached perspective of a dream. The opening lines which describe the gushing of Usumacinta's headwaters evoke feelings of remoteness in time, of primordial beginnings. The image of this great river moving through time and space becomes the central symbol and metaphoric undergirding for the poem.

As Francisco Pabón has pointed out, "El canto del Usumacinta" is a fusion of myth and history. Thus on one level Pellicer uses the image of the river as a point of departure to narrate the fall of the Mayan empire:

> Afterward the land was submerged
> and the sacred corn rotted
> and in the empty cities
> the reign of the orchids began.

> Después fueron los paisajes sumergidos
> y el sagrado maíz se pudrió
> y en las ciudades desalojadas
> el reinado de las orquídeas se inició.
>
> (475)

On another, more symbolic plane, the narrator becomes the embodiment of pre-Columbian man. For example the man-tree motif appears again in the sixth stanza, integrated into an important visual image:

> And I was a large tropical tree.
> I had birds on my head
> and a jaguar at my feet
> . . . .

In me, the primordial forces have made love:
Fire, air, land and sea.

Yo era un gran árbol tropical.
En mi cabeza tuve pájaros;
sobre mis piernas un jaguar.
. . . .
En mí se han amado las fuerzas de origen:
el fuego y el aire, la tierra y el mar.

                                                    (472)

While in the past we have seen many poems in which Pellicer has
tried to duplicate the effects of landscape painters, here there is an
interesting parallel with pre-Columbian art. The unusual figure of
the tree surrounded on the top by birds and on one side with a
jaguar is suggestive of a basic technique in Nahuatl artistic language:
the use of animal imagery to exemplify the unification of opposites.
The appearance of the ubiquitous tree image together with the four
primordial elements in the same stanza adds another dimension to
the poem. As scholars of pre-Hispanic art have pointed out, the tree
of life is a basic symbol of cosmic unity in Nahuatl thought.

In the closing stanzas of the poem, we once again encounter a
reference to synthetic union:

You are the water of my land. . . .
Man within you is now a rock which speaks
between the animal and vegetable kingdoms
Through a hole in a decomposed tree
passes the green silence of a Quetzal. . . .

Eres el agua grande de mi tierra. . . .
El hombre en ti es ahora la piedra que habla
entre el reino animal y el reino vegetal.
Por el hueco de un árbol podrido
pasa el verde silencio del quetzal. . . .

                                                    (476)

The reference to the Quetzal bird in the last line serves to reinforce
the earlier scattered references to cosmic unity (the intermingling of
the elements) for Quetzalcoatl, the god of life, was the primordial

figure in Nahuatl mythology and a cardinal symbol in the concept of material transfiguration and solar harmony.

Next to these myth-related pieces the poems dedicated to hero figures (Morelos, Bolívar, Justo Sierra, Cuauhtémoc, and José Gervasio Artigas) are the most thematically related group of poems. Perhaps "Tempestad y calma en honor de Morelos" ("Storm and Calm in Honor of Morelos") is the most successful of these compositions. As the title hints, the poem is divided into two parts: the first a grandiloquent and hyperbolic eulogy of the Mexican liberator and the second a subdued portrait of Morelos as an adolescent. It is interesting to note that Pellicer's interest in social equality, first sounded in *Piedra de sacrificios* in 1924, appears again in this collection. Thus Morelos is depicted less as a great martial figure than as a personification of social justice:

> Glory to you because you made Blacks, Indians and white men equal
> Glory to you, Mexican, and Continental man
> Glory to you who impoverished the rich.
>
> Gloria a ti, al igualar indios, negros y blancos
> Gloria y ti, mexicano y hombre continental.
> Gloria a ti que empobreciste a los ricos. . . .
>
> (462)

There are at least two other poems which merit special attention in *Subordinaciones:* "Nocturno a mi madre" ("Nocturne to my Mother") and "Tema para un Nocturno" ("Theme for a Nocturne"). "Nocturno a mi madre" is not only of interest from a biographical point of view (in that it clearly shows Pellicer's unusual devotion to his mother), but stylistically it signals a departure from his traditional concern with visual imagery. Instead of the accustomed buoyant or epic qualities, the tone of this poem is dreamy and pensive. Pellicer directly addresses the reader: "A moment ago/ my mother and I stopped praying" ("Hace un momento/ mi madre y yo dejamos de rezar" [457]) and on the basis of this simple statement develops the remainder of the poem. With alternating long and short syllable lines he first constructs a portrait of his mother's qualities and finally in the last two stanzas establishes an identification between his own somnolence and the dreams of his sleeping mother, with perhaps a hint of her eventual demise.

The last poem "Tema para un nocturno" continues the reflective
mood set in "Nocturno a mi madre." It is structured around an
unusual theme in Pellicer: the coming of death. As if to reaffirm his
identification with nature and light he declares here that:

It will have to look for me in the trees and among the clouds
. . . .
I cannot wait for it: I have a date with life, with brightness and song.

Y ha de buscarme sobre los árboles y entre las nubes
. . . .
yo no puedo esperarla: tengo una cita
con la vida, a las luces de un cantar.

                                                                            (477)

The elegiac mood of the last two poems in *Subordinaciones* was an
augury of the direction Pellicer's verse was to take in *Práctica de
vuelo (Practice of Flight,* 1956) a collection of eighty-seven mostly
laudatory and devotional sonnets. It is impossible to consider *Práctica de vuelo* as marking a definite phase of Pellicer's career, because
the book consists of poems written from as early as 1929 to as late as
1952. In particular, one group of poems dealing with the Virgin
Mary appeared in 1940 under the title *Ara virginum.*

III   Practice of Flight

The poems in *Práctica de vuelo (Practice of Flight)* are arranged in
rough chronological order under a series of fifteen thematic subti-
tles. In the first sonnet, "Soneto a causa de mi tercer viaje a Palestina" ("Sonnet on my third trip to Palestine"), the poet voices the
same query he raised in "Deseos" ("Desires") of *6, 7 poemas:* "Lord,
why do I again take your landscapes/ into my arms?" ("Por qué,
Señor, a tus paisajes tomo/ de nuevo entre mis brazos?" [481]). This
technique of beginning a poem with a formulaic supplication to the
Divine is used repeatedly in *Práctica de vuelo,* particularly in those
poems grouped under the heading, "Sonetos dolorosos" ("Sonnets
of Sorrow"). The already familiar tendency to concretize the
abstract, with a special emphasis on the sense experiences, is readily
apparent in this opening poem.

The third stanza exemplifies yet another basic stylistic feature of
this collection. This is the use of parallel but opposing images of
lightness and darkness, hardness and softness, to underscore both

the physical and spiritual distance between the poet and the Creator.

> The cradle and the grave. Stone and sky.
> Landscape of Israel. A fecund thirst.
> Stonelike Samaria. . . .
>
> La cuna y el Sepulcro. Piedra y cielo.
> Paisajes de Israel. La sed fecunda
> La Samaria de piedra. . . .

(481)

This basic antithesis, expressed mainly through images of color and to a lesser degree by tactile imagery, is a cardinal feature of *Práctica de vuelo*.

This initial poem is followed by a series of three sonnets brought together under the heading, "Sonetos bajo el signo de la cruz" ("Sonnets under the sign of the cross") and dated January 23, 1940. The three poems are closely interrelated and as a whole have a perceptible poetic structure which can be described as moving from the concrete gradually to the abstract. The first poem opens with an explicit visual image of the poet stretching his arms out in the shape of a cross.

> I stretched out my arms
> and the human cross
> that my body became, drank in the
> essence of heaven and earth. . . .
>
> Alcé los brazos y la cruz humana
> que fue mi cuerpo así, cielos y tierra
> en su sangre alojó. . . .

(482)

The autobiographical, reflective tone is continued in the second sonnet in which the poet recounts a moment of religious-aesthetic truth. Alone one night in the Holy Land, the poet yearns to be able to express the glory of the Creator through the medium of language and directly addresses his muse: "poetry look, be silent, come" ("poesía, mira, calla, ven" [483]). In the third poem, the emphasis shifts back to the central image of the first sonnet when Pellicer

draws an explicit comparison between his desire for spiritual perfection and inner peace and a tree reaching its branches toward the
life-giving rays of the sun.

> If I could only lift my arms
> and open them like the ripe fruit
> of a tree toward the Sun!

> Si yo pudiera levantar los brazos
> y abrirlos como en fruto bien maduro
> hace el árbol al sol!

(483)

In short, these three poems form a single extended meditation on
the theme of spiritual perfection and are linked by a central visual
impression which progresses from a specific, pictorial figure of the
poet stretching his arms in the shape of a cross to a more symbolic
plane of the man-tree image.

This sonnet trilogy is followed by another group of three poems
entitled "Sonetos lamentables" ("Lamentable Sonnets") which were
written in the prison of San Diego, Tacubaya in February, 1930. In
short, the poems are a chronicle of spiritual liberation and redemption. In the first poem, the author underscores his own state of
imperfection through a series of antithetical images. The second
sonnet displays a greater sense of self-esteem and is clearly more
outward directed in its point of view. The tone of morbid self-
introspection of the first poem has given way to an assertive search
for God. In the final poem, the same motif is extended as Pellicer
continues to stress the intermingling of the Creator with the
Created. Union with the Divine is thus described in terms of the
motion and energy of certain natural phenomena—the flowing of
water, the blowing of wind:

> When Hope disappears and
> Faith and Charity alone make their presence felt.
> One will be able to walk on water.

> Desaparezca la Esperanza y solas
> la Fe y la Caridad dejen sus huellas.
> Se podrá caminar sobre las olas.

(488)

This propensity for antithetical imagery is evidenced in Pellicer's "Sonetos de la esperanza" ("Sonnets of Hope"). The theme of the two sonnets, the spiritual imperfection of man, is reinforced through a series of visual contrasts. Adjectives and verbs of light are applied to the Creator while the poetic narrator states that he lives in a world of shadows. This same theme is continued in the two "Sonetos de la Luz" ("Sonnets of light"). Much like the "Sonetos bajo el signo de la cruz" ("Sonnets under the sign of the cross"), the two "Sonnets of light" are inextricably related. However, in opposition to the former, these poems are developed along a trajectory of increasing visual concreteness. The first sonnet aludes to the central theme of the omnipresence of Christ but does so on a level of greater linguistic abstraction than that of the second poem. Suggestive images ("thickness of silence" and "the light that cannot be hidden") give way to more specific visual referents as the poet compares himself to a massive tropical ceiba tree reaching toward the sun.

Pellicer's strong attraction for the natural world is evidenced again in the four-sonnet group labeled "Sonetos todo un día" ("Sonnets All Day"). In the first, Pellicer describes what might best be called a poetic fantasy when he muses that for a moment he has escaped the bonds of terrestrial reality and become a cloud. "I am a cloud which rises up like a volcano" ("y soy nube que en volcán se iza" [143]). In the second, the omniscient poetic narrator continues his adulation of the beauties of landscape, but now the vital life-force of nature is described as a tactile experience. The poem ends with a supplication to the Creator to elevate the poet to a higher plane of spiritual perfection. In the final sonnet, Pellicer refers back to the central dream image of the first poem: "If I again could be the Angel that I was" ("¡Si yo pudiera ser el ángel que fui!" [495]) and links this fantasy to a more general observation on the nature of cosmic harmony. As we have seen before, there is a constant and repeated equation of man to nature, of the part to the whole, in Pellicer's verse. Thus, the poem ends with the reappearance of the man-tree image: "And I sing amid arrogance and excess/ knowing that I am but a splinter of the oak tree . . ." ("Y entre soberbias y lujurias canto/ sabiendo que del roble soy astilla . . ." [495]).

The "Sonetos suplicantes" ("Supplicatory Sonnets") are in many ways similar to the "Sonetos todo un día." This two-sonnet grouping begins with an autobiographical reflection which extends to a symbolic portrayal of the interpenetration of man and the natural world.

In the first stanza, the poet recalls a moment of spiritual introspection he once experienced in Assisi. The moment is described in the second stanza but the persona now emerges as part of the cosmic harmony:

> I was a corporal oak-tree; a singing evergreen.
> . . . .
> I looked in my heart: It was a chasm
> And when I cast out the inertia, I became divine.
>
> Fui roble corporal; cantante encino
> . . . .
> Me miré el corazón: ya estaba hondo;
> y al vaciarlo de inercia fui divino.
>
> (499)

If an emphasis on images of brightness and luminesence is the major feature of the poems we have studied thus far in *Práctica de vuelo*, then the opposite would be true of the two "Sonetos nocturnos" ("Nocturnal Sonnets"). The title alone calls to mind the well-known solipsistic verses of Pellicer's close friend Xavier Villaurrutia. In contrast to the rather easily perceptible structure and metaphoric clarity of the majority of the poems in this book, the "Sonetos nocturnos" are works of greater complexity. The problem of time and more specifically, immortality, emerges as the central focus of these sonnets. The first poem begins with an image of suspended time similar to the one encountered in "Uxmal":

> I am Time between two eternities.
> Before me eternity, and after me eternity. Fire;
> A single shadow between two immense lights.
>
> Tiempo soy entre dos eternidades.
> Antes de mi la eternidad y luego
> de mí, la eternidad. El fuego;
> sombra sola entre inmensas claridades.
>
> (502)

The poet resolves the problem of his mortality in the third stanza when he affirms that man achieves eternal life through God. Once again the experience of the Absolute is translated into a vivid pictorial image dominated by the figure of the living ceiba tree, whose branches are plucked by the Divine. In the final stanza the poet evokes an image of timelessness parallel to the one which opened the poem. Here, however, there is an emphasis on enduring continuance:

> I am time; the beginning and the end,
> Time which does not die and does not kill
> Tempered by the zenith and the light.

> Tiempo soy, tiempo último y primero,
> el tiempo que no muere y que no mata,
> templado de cenit y de lucero.

> (502)

The low-key reflective tone set in "Sonetos nocturnos" is projected as well in a collection of eleven sonnets entitled "Nocturno" ("Nocturne") which recounts an emotional experience of a single evening. They are much like the "Sonetos todo un día" inasmuch as they are centered about a series of related impressions. In the first poem, the poet sketches the figure of a lone man gazing into the fathomless night. This is followed in the third stanza by an apostrophe to the Creator: "Lord and Master, my solitude is an urn/ in which I place the pearl which adores you" ("Dios y Señor, mi soledad es urna/ donde instalo la perla de adorarte" [503]). The poems which follow are by and large descriptions of landscapes in which the poet sees the reflection of his own solitude.

The second sonnet in "Nocturnos" opens with an important visual image which calls to mind the poet's repeated efforts to fuse the figure of man with various manifestations of the natural world:

> Foot of night, hand of dawn,
> zenith-like head . . .
> my fluvial voice is planted
> in the powerful presence of nature.

> Pie de la noche, mano de la aurora,
> cabeza cenital . . .
> toda mi voz fluvial dada en plantío;
> poderosa presencia agricultura.

> (504)

In the last stanza a reference is made to a moment of poetic truth, a period of animated suspension when the poet will be able to fuse with the whole and be one with nature: ". . . in that hour/ when all the clocks have stopped/ already a bit timeless and deserted" (". . . en esa hora/ de todos los relojes detenida/ ya un poco intemporal y desertora" [504]).

In sonnets three through six, Pellicer continues to inventory the rich and multifaceted texture of the landscapes he recalls in this poetic revery. The outstanding feature of these sonnets, which in many ways call to mind the travel poems of *Camino*, is the author's propensity to personify nature. Pellicer speaks of "the nakedness of the field, its sonorous musculature" and addresses himself to "young autumn." There is, however, a considerable shift in tone from the seventh sonnet onward where the theme of solitude becomes predominant. Thus the poet exclaims: "Solitude has seen . . . the ruin of my torrid cities" ("La soledad ha visto. . . . La ruina de mis tórridas ciudades" [506]). In the eighth sonnet, he addresses the Virgin Mary, decrying the superficiality of his poetic experience and beseeching her to let him drink of the water of poetic inspiration:

> Let me drink from the nutritive waters
> which in each sip have the aroma
> of roses and the shimmering of stars.
>
> Dame a beber del agua sustanciosa
> que en cada sorbo tiene de la rosa
> y de la estrella aroma y alhajero.
>
> (507)

The poet's all-consuming solitude and longing to be one with God reach a peak in the last three sonnets of this group. The persona laments with growing intensity the bareness of his existence. The visually concrete and sensuous animal and vegetable images of the earlier sonnets have given way to tropes of darkness and despair. On both a philosophical and visual plane the last sonnet resolves the conflict which has plagued the poet when suddenly the narrator feels his body invaded pore by pore by the gleaming force of the divine trinity.

The introspective nature and subtle images of the "Sonetos nocturnos" stand in contrast to the three "Sonetos fraternales" ("Fraternal Sonnets") which were dedicated to the Mexican poet Jaime

Sabines and dated August 29, 1948. The second sonnet in the group is particularly noteworthy, because in very specific language it casts the central motif in Pellicer's poetry of the sun as the primordial center of life. As we have already pointed out in our discussion of the four elements, the sun was an important image in pre-Columbian thought because it was considered to be the force which gave life to the universe. The "Sonetos fraternales" are followed in *Práctica de vuelo* by the twelve "Sonetos para el altar de La Virgin" ("Sonnets for the Altar of the Virgin") which in turn, are further subdivided into groups of four poems under the following titles: "Ave María," "Mater Amabilis," "Mater Admirabilis," and "Regina Caeli." This group of poems is dated May and June, 1940. These divisions correspond to the four cardinal moments of the Virgin's life: the Annunciation, the Nativity, the Passion, and the Assumption of Mary to Heaven. The poems which comprise "Mater Amabilis" describe the Nativity of Christ. The techniques used by Pellicer here are reminiscent of some of his earlier travel poems where he was trying to evoke a definite picture with words. The images are elemental and are linked by the comments of the poet-narrator as if he were describing the arrangement of figures in a painting.

> The Virgin softly sings to the child Jesus.
> It begins to dawn. The grass grows
> with happy humility. The saintly night
>
> sleeps and dreams. The shepherds leave.
> The arrival of an angel shakes
> a hill, which changes color.
>
> La Virgen en sordina al Niño canta.
> Comienza a amanecer. La yerba crece
> con alegre humildad. La noche santa
>
> duerme . . . sueña. Se marchan los pastores.
> La llegada de un ángel estremece
> la colina, que cambia de colores.
>
> (515)

The sonnets portraying the Assumption ("Regina Caeli") are in general more abstract and less visually specific than the poems

which preceded them. The first poem in the group is particularly
provocative, since it contains an enumeration of sense images. Just
as Mary has ascended to heaven so the poet yearns to rise toward
the Creator. Thus he longs for the ineffable, for eyes to see that
which has not been seen, and ears to hear that which has not been
spoken.

The poet's solitude and yearning to verbalize his feelings of humil-
ity and unworthiness with respect to the Creator are again voiced in
the six-sonnet series "Otros sonetos" ("Other Sonnets"). The first
poem begins with an image of confinement where the poet compares his isolation to the depths of an abandoned well. The same
motif is extended in the second sonnet where he speaks of "This
night lodged between the four/ walls of my life" ("Esta noche alojada
entre las cuatro/ paredes de mi vida" [522]) and which culminates
with only a hint of despairing solipsism: "The window closed and in
the extreme/ thickness of shadows, dead/ From the terror of not
being, I dream that I live" ("Se cerró la ventana y en la extrema
solidez de la sombra, todo muerto/ del terror de no estar, sueño que
vivo" [522]). Isolated and alone, the poet compares himself to a
hungry, orphaned dog. In the fifth sonnet, the poet narrator climac-
tically questions his destiny, asking where he should go. The answer
is revealing. It is through the medium of language, Pellicer in-
sinuates, that he will be able to break away from his spiritual isolation and relate to the Creator.

The largest group of poems in *Práctica de vuelo* is the twenty-five
"Sonetos dolorosos" ("Sorrowful Sonnets"). Here, Pellicer continues
to implore divine recognition and comments tangentially on the
human condition. An important feature of these poems is the fre-
quent use of antithetical color images of lightness and darkness
which are employed to emphasize the spiritual and physical distance
between man and his Creator. The theme of poetry also surfaces in
this collection. For example, in the thirteenth sonnet Pellicer again
laments the limitations of his artistic experience. He now yearns to
escape from a world of bright, visual images and turn to an examination of his soul: "I want my eyes in my soul now" ("Quiero los ojos en
el alma ahora" [532]). Here as well, there crops up a reference to the
anti-intellectual nature of his poetry: "I know nothing about myself, I
only sing/ and I don't know what I sing" ("Yo nada sé de mi, ya sólo
canto/ y no sé lo que canto" [536]).

This poem dated September, 1950, seems to mark a rather subtle thematic division in this series, since the sonnets which follow are characterized by a more intense desire to achieve a union or fusion with the Divine. The sixteenth sonnet, for example, is probably the one which most clearly betrays the influence of the Spanish mystics (above all Saint John of the Cross) with its emphasis on an all-consuming passion to be one with God: "I am burning up in a dark fire/ and I live only to see you one day" ("Me estoy quemando en un oscuro fuego/ y por verte algún día sólo existo" [533]).

In the following poem we find an even more clearly defined reference to the type of experience for which the poet yearns, and it becomes clear that Pellicer is not a true mystic, for the spiritual reality after which he yearns is one fully apparent to the senses. In fact, it is postulated as an almost wholly tactile, sensuous phenomenon. Thus, in the eighteenth sonnet the poet pleads for a synesthetic moment when he will be able to more fully feel the Creator's presence:

> Let the senses you give me mingle
> in a single sensation and thus recall
> your forgotten beauty. . . .

> Que los sentidos que me das concuerden
> en un solo sentir y así recuerden
> tu olvidada belleza escarnecida . . .

(534)

In the final stanza, Pellicer moves to yet another level of perception by employing an important aquatic image. It is now no longer through the mere human senses that he seeks communion with the Divine but, as we have seen repeatedly, by a transformation into a part of nature's harmonic whole: "when you go by, you will hear a little brook/ which happily calls to you amid its sad song" ("Cuando pases, oirás que un arroyuelo/ te llama entre su canto triste" [534]).

As we have seen before, Pellicer has persistently related his perception of Divine experience to animal and vegetable life. He has declared himself to be "a strong animal" and on many occasions, a ceiba tree. He has said that he sees with the "eyes of a fish," that his voice is "fluvial," and that his gaze has the "dew of an orchard."

In the twenty-second sonnet, the theme of poetry appears again. It is presented as a reconciling force in Pellicer's attempt to come to grips with the ineffable:

Will victory approach invisibly?
Eternal youth, Poetry
begins to dawn amid the slag.

¿Se acercará invisible la victoria?
Joven de eternidad, la Poesía
comienza a amanecer entre la escoria.

(536)

The dual themes of poetry and the search for the Absolute are deftly joined in this last poem when the poet declares that one day he will seek the Divine in order to become "The craftsman of your words." *Práctica de vuelo* closes with a miscellany of five sonnets, all of which are dated with the exception of the final piece entitled "A Cristo." Written later than the majority of the poems, these selections demonstrate a marked tone of pessimism and despair. The poet feels disoriented and frequently employs images of decay and putrification.

Since it is a commonplace among Pellicer's critics to apply the term "mystic" to his poetry, it is important that a number of basic distinctions be made before further discussing this aspect of his verse. Essentially, mysticism refers to an attitude of mind which accepts intuition as a guide for understanding the Absolute and regards matter as impeding the soul's quest for union with the Divine. Simply stated, the mystic is one who seeks direct communion with God through subjective experience.

The problem of Pellicer's "mysticism" must be approached with care. It is true that occasionally he uses imagery popular with the Spanish mystics and expresses a desire for union with the Creator. However, Pellicer is not a mystic in the technical sense of the word. It might be convenient to say that Pellicer's attitude is really more that of a Christian pantheist, since the Creator is almost always equated with nature. As we have seen, the compositions in *Práctica de vuelo* hinge on the basic tenet that the divinity of the Creator can be perceived in and identified with the external world in its entirety—sky, sea, sun, and flora and fauna. Unlike the mystics who plotted a careful course along the road to the ultimate union, Pellicer makes only fleeting and indirect references to such an experience. J. M. Cohen characterized *Práctica de vuelo* best when he spoke of "a decorative piety, an unmetaphysical praise of the Lord seen in the light and color of His Creation."[3]

CHAPTER 9

Recent Poetry

Práctica de vuelo was the last major book-length collection of verse brought out by Pellicer before the publication of the *Material poético 1918–1961 (Poetic Materials)* in 1962 by the National University of Mexico Press which contains all his previously published poems together with thirty-two selections which had not been published before. The same year Pellicer published *Con palabras y fuego (With Words and Fire)*, an extension of his "Oda a Cuauhtémoc" ("Ode to Cuauhtémoc") which has already been discussed in relation to *Piedra de sacrificios*. It would be difficult, if not impossible, to meaningfully discuss the uncollected poems which close this edition of his complete works. Because of the great diversity of themes in these uncollected pieces together with the poems Pellicer has published from 1962 to 1970, we have chosen to study this poetry by major thematic clusters: (1) social protest and indigenous poetry; (2) religious verse, confessional poems; and (3) occasional poetry.

Pellicer's poetry has reflected two recurrent tendencies: a search for beauty and a call to decry social injustice. This social or civic bent has surfaced with regularity during Pellicer's long career as a creative writer, but was particularly evident in *Piedra de sacrificios (Sacrificial Stone)*. There are at least eight poems from his more recent works which could be classified as socially committed: "Discurso a Cananea" ("Discourse for Cananea"), "Cien líneas para ti" ("A Hundred Lines for You"), "A Juárez" ("To Juárez"), "Las estrofas a José Martí" ("Strophes to José Martí"), "Toda América nuestra" ("All America, Ours"), "Líneas por el Che Guevara" ("Lines for Che Guevara"), "Surgente fin" ("Surging End") and "Teotihuacán y 13 de agosto" ("Teotihuacán and the 13th of August").

123

I *The Protest Poems*

The undated "Discurso a Cananea" calls to mind Pellicer's intense and hyperbolic protest verse of the 1920s. The long poem has fifteen stanzas and one hundred lines of verse and describes the appalling working conditions in the copper mines of Cananea in the state of Sonora, Mexico. The objects of Pellicer's wrath are the oligarchic dictators of Latin America: Marcos Pérez Jiménez (Venezuela), Rafael Leónidas Trujillo (Dominican Republic), Anastasio Somoza (Nicaragua), Fulgencio Batista (Cuba), Gustavo Rojas Pinilla (Colombia), and Carlos Castillo Armas (Guatemala). He calls them "Fat pigs who sniff amidst blood and treason" ("Grandes puercos que hocean entre la sangre y la traición" [581]) and criticizes the idle rich who squander their fortunes with petty and trivial pleasures. "Discurso a Cananea," while clearly propagandistic, is not unpoetic. As a rhetorical work, it has a grandiloquent and dazzling appeal that builds slowly from an indefinite reference to blood as the fluid of life in the first three stanzas to a more specific and direct allusion to "blood hidden behind the face/ of the broken miner" ("la sangre oculta en la mirada/ del minero dilapidado" [580]). Pellicer spoke about the poem in an interview with George O. Melnykovich: "I have always made a distinction between a poem and *poetry*. This is really a political poem in which some poetry occasionally enters. I don't consider that it's a poetic text. It's a political poem. When people talk about political poetry I have to laugh. Poetry isn't politics. It can't be. Politics is transitory . . . poetry is a permanent mysterious force."[1]

Similar to the "Discurso a Cananea" is "Cien líneas para ti" ("A Hundred Lines for You"). This eight-stanza poem dated Caracas, 1960, culminates a long series of poems and references to Simón Bolívar, the man whom Pellicer most admires. As in so many of Pellicer's poems, the first stanza serves as a general introduction to set the tone and establish the poet's point of view. The persona directly addresses the reader, telling him that today he had visited Bolívar's tomb. In the second stanza, the poet-narrator continues the same autobiographical thread, describing how yesterday he had taken a leaf from a giant rain-tree. In the next lines, Pellicer suddenly shifts from an objective narrative perspective to a more complex plane of metaphoric thought when he writes: "and upon returning to Caracas, I stripped off my leaves with sadness and joy" ("Y al volver a Caracas me deshojé en tristezas y alegrías" [633]). This propensity for sudden shifts in perspective is one of Pellicer's techniques which elevates his poetry from a level of commonplace to one of innovation. The appearance of the man-tree motif in Pellicer's verse is not unexpected. In the third stanza the poet augurs the emotional outburst which surfaces in the fourth stanza by referring to clouds which have begun to darken the sky. The fourth stanza is a diatribe against the dictators Rafael Leonidas Trujillo and Anastasio Somoza. The poem concludes with a challenge to Latin Americans to unite and fight injustice: "Let us unite . . ./ and give ourselves to the fight/ against all injustice" ("deberemos reunir nuestras briznas/ y entregarnos a la lucha/ contra toda injusticia" [635]).

The Cuban patriot José Martí (1853–1895) also became an object of praise and a point of departure for an attack on social injustice in "Las estrofas a José Martí" ("Strophes to José Martí"). Pellicer addresses the Cuban martyr and decries the plight of the downtrodden Latin American community of nations by exclaiming: "Free us from science/ in the hands of despots and millionaires!" ("Líbranos de la ciencia/ en manos de los déspotas y de los millonarios!" [604]).

Not all of Pellicer's social verse was as vitriolic and direct as the poems just discussed. "A Juárez" ("To Juárez"), a group of three undated sonnets, is a civic hymn which expresses pride in Mexico's national heritage. The first poem is a generalized eulogy of Benito Juáréz (1806–1872), a pure blood Zapotec Indian who was President of Mexico from 1857 to 1872. In the second sonnet, through a cluster of vegetable images, the life of the patriot is compared to the growth of an ear of corn, and in the third selection, a comparison is drawn between the glories of Mexico's pre-Columbian past and the exploits of Juárez.

A muted cry for Latin American unity is sounded in "Toda América nuestra" and "Líneas por el Che Guevara." "Toda América nuestra" is a sonnet which alludes to the union of the autochthonous and Western European cultures in the Americas. In the final tercet, Pellicer juxtaposes both pre-Hispanic and Western religious symbols, insinuating that from a union of these different but complementary philosophies a new hope for Latin America will spring: "Bell tower and pyramid join" ("Campanario a pirámide se alía"), he exclaims.

In his "Líneas por el Che Guevara" ("Lines for Che Guevara"),

Pellicer once again took up the banner of Latin American unity. The poem was written for a special issue of the prestigious Mexican journal, *Cuadernos Americanos,* dedicated to the memory of Ernesto "Che" Guevara, a communist revolutionary killed in Bolivia in 1967. Unlike many of Pellicer's earlier poems of social comment, his "Líneas por el Che Guevara" is muted and controlled. There are no fiery attacks against economic imperialism but rather a restrained call for Latin American unity. Pellicer discussed the broader implications of the poem in an interview with this writer in 1972. When asked about the opening lines of the last stanza: "We are at the dawning of the nations/ who want to be one nation" ("Estamos en la aurora de los pueblos/ que quieren ser un solo pueblo"), he replied: "Well I am referring to the fact that already in the last few years, the peoples of Latin America are beginning to realize that it is necessary to know each other and that without this union we shall never be a great continental force. In short, Simón Bolívar's ideas are still alive. But you used the word 'Pan-American' and we should like the union to include both Americas. However, the economic imperialism of the United States has prevented it. We have nothing against the North American people, but we do complain about the conduct of United States' economic imperialism. I hope very much that in our America, that someday, which I will probably not see, there will be a community of people among the great North American nation and the Latin American peoples."

While almost all of Pellicer's socially oriented verse is concerned with Latin America, there is one curious exception: "Surgente fin" ("Surging End"), which deals with the primordial ties between Africa and Mexico. The two cultures are linked, Pellicer notes, by a similar rich religious-mythic past and by the fact that they have both been victims of the economic imperialism of Europe and the United States. Pellicer's interest in black culture is no anomaly, for he knew the black American poet Langston Hughes well. He was also equally well acquainted with the black Cuban poet Nicolás Guillén, whom he met in Spain during the Spanish Civil War. Two of Pellicer's friends in the *Contemporáneos* group, Salvador Novo and Xavier Villaurrutia, had written pioneer articles on black poetry in the United States which were published in the journal *Contemporáneos* in the late 1920s and the early 1930s.

"Surgente fin" is not, however, merely a protest against the mistreatment of the dark-skinned peoples. The fact that Pellicer chose

Africa rather than black America as his point of departure is significant. Clearly, Pellicer was eager to point out—and here the influence of José Vasconcelos is obvious—that the tropical peoples are united in almost mystic-archetypal terms around the figure of the sun: "In Africa and America the sun forged two cultures: Thebes died by day; Palenque is seen but in shadows" ("En África y América el sol quemó culturas:/ Tebas murió de día; Palenque se ve a oscuras" [586]). "Surgente fin" is also intriguing from a structural and stylistic point of view. The poem begins in much the same way as "Uxmal" and "El canto del Usumacinta." There is a gradual process of mythification, a subtle change in perspective by which the poet-narrator moves to a plane of greater omniscience. For example, the first two stanzas are constructed with a deliberately vague and suggestive cluster of images which lead in the third stanza to a reference to "the river of the night," a period of time to which the poet pays hommage:

> Because it gave me the will to fight
> My blood boiled and my muscles trembled
> I was but an athlete surrounded by twilight.

> Porque dio a mis arterias bríos de pugilato
> y calenté mi sangre y desbordé mis músculos.
> No fui sino un atleta cercado de crepúsculos.
>
> (585)

The reference first to "river of night" and then "shadow of night" suggests the coming of sleep and the subsequent uncensored world of dreams. It prepares the reader to accept what will follow. We have seen this technique often before in any number of constructions. The poet begins gazing into the night sky which quickly leads him to some form of poetic meditation. Here, however, the suggested state of somnolence is directly linked to some type of unconscious or archetypal level of thought from which the poet emerges as the all-seeing incarnation of primitive man. In the opening lines of the fourth stanza, the poet states:

> But something, a living dream of antiquity
> resurrects in my blood a timeless glory.
> And he who loved eternal youth in silence
> now drinks at the water's edge the immense
> fraternal light. . . .

Pero algo, un sueño vivo de antigüedad actual
reorganiza en mi sangre su gloria intemporal.
Y quien amó en silencio la juventud eterna,
hoy bebe a flor del agua la inmensa luz fraterna.

(585)

What follows is a combination of flashy visual images ("oceans of chlorophyll") describing the flora and fauna of Africa and references to the important role the continent will play in the future of the world: "Africa is a mirror of what will happen" ("El África es espejo de lo que va a pasar" [586]). In the ninth stanza, Pellicer concretizes the abstract feelings of union or affinity with the black peoples he has alluded to when he states:

I have drops of Black blood in my veins, I feel
rivers and trees growing, I feel myself linked
to the thirst of the desert. . . .

Tengo en mi sangre gotas de sangre negra, siento
crecer ríos y árboles, unificarme, siento
el desierto de sed que en mi destino instala. . . .

(587)

Then in his characteristic style, the poet gradually records his transformation into a living part of the tropical landscape:

I hear in my body the roar of a humming workshop
I am a bustling lumberyard.
my nose and mouth
are but fruits hanging from the boardlike
trees of the jungle.

oigo en mi cuerpo el río de un taller que trabaja
soy un campo de acción. En mi maderería
el tablón de la selva tiene de frutería
mi nariz y mi boca.

(588)

The conceits used to depict this process of compenetration with the natural world are similar to the mystical and magical metaphors described by Hermann Pongs in that they are essentially de-animizing. There is a shift from the world of men to that of things and vice versa. In the middle of this same stanza, there is a change in direction as the poet redirects the focus of the poem outward by addressing the Creator in a plea for Christian understanding. The poem ends with a strong and graphic appeal to the Divine: "Lord, let . . . me see/ my hand burning like a living Torch" ("Haz Señor, que . . . yo vea:/ que mi mano se queme como antorcha viva" [589]).

Tangentially related to the poems of social protest is Pellicer's *Teotihuacán y 13 de agosto: Ruina de Tenochtitlán.* The poem was prefaced by the following statement by the author: "This poem was written for the ceremony celebrating the reconstruction of a part of the archeological zone of Teotihuacán and read by its author in a solemn act which took place in front of the pyramid of the Moon the morning of September 17, 1964, in the presence of Adolfo López Mateos, then President of Mexico. The last 13 lines are dedicated to President López Mateos and allude to his extraordinary governmental work."[2] The place names alluded to in the title are important ones in Mexican history. Teotihuacán, which means City of the Gods in Nahuatl, is the oldest city in Meso-America and is located some fifty kilometers from Mexico City. Tenochtitlán is the Aztec name for the area which is presently Mexico City and was, before the arrival of the Spaniards in 1519, the seat of the Aztec empire.

Within the context of Pellicer's mythologically oriented poems, "Teotihuacán" is a work of enormous importance, for much like *Con palabras y fuego*, it underscores his constant effort to reinterpret the cosmologies of ancient Mexico in the light of twentieth-century realities. Few critics have studied the poem in any depth, with the exception of Francisco Pabón, who sees the work as central to the understanding of Pellicer's peculiar vision of the universe. For Pabón, "Teotihuacán" is a tightly organized evocation of an entire complex of pre-Columbian symbols, the most important of which is the figure of the pyramid which serves as the central image of the whole composition: "As can be seen, the images are constructed on the basis of both a real and symbolic structure—the five cardinal points—which acts like an invisible axis whose movement configures the geometric contours of the pyramid, from the horizontal base to the idea of the zenith."[3]

Similar to "Uxmal," the "Esquemas para una oda tropical," and the "Canto del Usumacinta," "Teotihuacán" is a poem of epic proportions. The opening lines focus immediately on the imposing geometric and symbolic figure of the pyramid with a definite physical and symbolic motion upward in the poem's first lines: "The word pyramid, touched by Heaven,/ lifts our arms and raises our eyes" ("La palabra pirámide, tocada por el cielo,/ levanta nuestos brazos y eleva nuestros ojos" [1]). Thus Pellicer, as he has done so often before, establishes an almost immediate attitude or tone which might be called mythic distance. In earlier poems such as "Surgente fin," the poet coaxes the reader into accepting the ritual or mythic orientation of the work by establishing a perspective of omniscience. Thus under the guise of sleep, the poet-narrator assumes the stance of a seer. Here, there is no transition from the subjective persona to the objective and omniscient narrator, for through an immediate emphasis on symbolic geometrical form, the poet has already fixed the perspective of the poem and established its predominant tone. What quickly follows in the first stanza is the unraveling of a number of cardinal pre-Columbian myths depicted through a series of important Aztec totemic symbols:

> There are slowly crafted nights and days:
> the pyramid goes down and gives the sun to the moon.
> The sun, like the jaguar, moves silently.
> Hours are spots on his skin. . . .
> What a constellation of stars lives in this Heaven
> since the ancient Hero became a star!

> Hay noches como días, lánguidamente hechos:
> la pirámide baja y da sol a la Luna.
> Es tan jaguar el Sol, que pasa silencioso.
> Las horas son las manchas de su piel. . . .
> ¡Qué población de estrellas en este cielo vive
> desde que el Héroe antiguo se transformó en estrella!

(1)

It is probably no coincidence that the first allusion to a pre-Columbian diety is to Quetzalcoatl, the creator of the universe of man and the supreme magician of Aztec lore, to whom an important mural is dedicated at Teotihuacán. The specific reference is to the rebirth of Quetzalcoatl as a star corresponding to the cyclical disappearance of Venus out of the Western sky and its reappearance in the East.

In the second and third stanzas there is an emphasis, somewhat parallel to that of the opening lines, on the symbolic importance of space, line, and volume. This technique seems to be an extension or culmination of Pellicer's earlier obsession with framing his portrait poems and playing optical games with color and geometric shapes and proportions:

> Man left here clear volume:
> he linked the horizon to the mountains. . . .
> There is a geometry whose rhythm joins
> the flowers of the day to the fruits of night
> Man loved peace in this enormous movement of
> volumes.

> El hombre dejó aquí los volúmenes claros:
> conjugó el horizonte con la montaña: . . .
> Hay una geometría cuyo ritmo congrega
> lo florido del día con el fruto nocturno.
> El hombre amó la paz en este enorme juego
> de volúmenes.

(2)

In the fourth stanza, Pellicer recounts the legend of the Creation, giving special attention again to the figure of Quetzalcoatl. While in the first stanza he was evoked as a fleeting symbol, here he emerges as an integral facet in the myth of creation, since in Aztec religious thought Quetzalcoatl symbolizes the vital synthesis of opposites which is the source of life. He is the archetype of man himself. After some thirteen lines describing Quetzalcoatl, Pellicer stresses the importance of language (poetry) as a catalyst from which creative energy and life spring:

> I return to the essence of pure and
> divine ideas. Elemental man discovers
> language amid the four elements.
> And now in sculpture, painting or words
> he communicates the soul of the highest things.

> Vuelvo a la desnudez de las ideas puras
> y divinas. El hombre descifra elemental
> la Lengua a la intemperie de los cuatro elementos.
> Y ya es en escultura, en pintura o palabras
> que comunica el alma de las cosas supremas.

(3)

Thus within the framework of the "law of the center" which has been previously discussed in conjunction with such poems as "Poema elemental," "Esquemas para una oda tropical," and "La voz," man and more specifically language (poetry) serves as a point of union from which creative energy and life spring. Pabón considers this an important juncture in the composition since, as he writes, "the poet situates himself within the emotive context of the poem and tells us to a certain extent what he is doing aesthetically in the work."[4]

The verses which follow move artfully away from a mythic, archetypal plane to a level of social concern. The thirty-fourth line of the fourth stanza marks the transition:

> Teotihuacán is a monument to the man of that time.
> Before Europe was the flower of civilization, Mexico
> gave marvelous blossoms to culture!
>
> Teotihuacán es honra del hombre y de su tiempo.
> Antes que Europa fuera flor de cultura, México
> flores de maravilla dio a la cultura!
>
> (4)

These lines stress the antiquity of Mexico's cultural heritage and introduce the last thirteen verses which eulogize the impressive program for social amelioration begun under Adolfo López Mateos. The motif of the four elements appears again but now cast within the mold of social reality: "Also the elements/ someday will be the cause of peace/ and not war . . ." ("También los elementos/ serán un día causa de paz y no de guerra" [5]). López Mateos becomes a symbol of the nation's emerging prosperity and an emblem of brotherhood and union:

> He who covered our land with roads and schools,
> and filled our spiritual needs, was able to tell the world
> Mexico exists, and lives. . . .
>
> Quien cubrió de caminos y escuelas nuestro espacio
> territorial y humano, salió al mundo a decirle:
> México existe, vive. . . .
>
> (5)

Published together with "Teotihuacán" was a related poem, "13 de Agosto: Ruina de Tenochtitlán," which begins with a tercet-refrain: "I am sad/ not because I'm a Mexican/ but because I'm a man" ("Me da tristeza/ no por mexicano/ sino sólo por hombre" [6]). The poem is an evocation of the ruins of the ancient Toltec city, narrated directly in the first person: "I am looking at the ruined city/ a flower crushed by a sinister foot" ("Estoy mirando la ciudad destruída,/ flor aplastada por un pie sombrío" [6]). This vision of the ruins of the ancient center of Toltec civilization leads to a more generalized and universal meditation on the futility of war and destruction:

> Well, yes ambition
> To destroy, to kill, to obtain and possess
> This is the reason for so much sorrow,
> so much ruin, so many hidden tears.
>
> Bueno, sí: ¡la ambición!
> Destruir, matar para obtener y poseer.
> Esta es la razón de tanto duelo,
> de tanta ruina, de tantas lágrimas oscuras.
>
> (7)

In the final verses of the second stanza, the poet hears amid the ruins the fluttering of a wounded eagle—a veiled reference perhaps to Quetzalcoatl who often was depicted as a winged serpent. The narrator continues his lament which climaxes with a graphic reference to the destruction of the pre-Columbian world:

> Out of the direction of Texcoco
> a storm is coming. I have
> nowhere to go. The flower of the
> four cardinal points has been stripped of its
> leaves. . . .
>
> Ya por el rumbo de Texcoco viene
> la tempestad y yo no tengo
> a donde ir. Se deshojó
> la flor de cuatro puntos cardinales. . . .
>
> (8–9)

The multilation of this central symbol in Aztec cosmology under-scores the poet's profound melancholy over the devastation of the seat of Toltec civilization. The reference here is again to the concept of the four cardinal points and the law of the center.

There are several other poems which, while not specifically "so-cially oriented," are related to the works just discussed in that they deal with important indigenous motifs. Pellicer's "Elegía apasion-ada" ("Passionate Elegy") is an example. It was written in commem-oration of the death of José Vasconcelos and dated June 30, 1960.

Although a long, discussive work, it merits attention for certain features of style. In the third stanza, for example, there is a curious reference to the four elements. Pellicer declares: "I was near this man/ in the earth and in the air, in fire and in water/ I witnessed the grandeur and the misery of his elements" ("Yo estuve cerca de este hombre/ en la tierra y en el aire, en el fuego y en el agua,/ yo presencié la grandeza y la miseria de sus elementos" [609]). Another trope which calls to mind Pellicer's debt to pre-Hispanic artistic imagery is the allusion in the seventh stanza to the union of fire and water through the paradoxical image of burning water. Pellicer wrote:

> When the master José Clemente Orozco
> painted his fire man in Guadalajara
> I, water from the torrid lands
> Thought, sun struck, of Vasconcelos.
>
> Cuando el maestro José Clemente Orozco
> pintó en Guadalajara su Hombre-Fuego,
> yo, agua de las tierras tórridas,
> pensé, todo quemado, en Vasconcelos.
>
> (610)

The union of opposites was at the basis of all creation, spiritual as well as material, in the Aztec world. Séjourné notes that "This spiritual principle is so basic that the Great Temple at Tenochtitlán was dedicated to it: the fact that the gods of rain and celestial fire were placed side by side at the top of the pyramid cannot be seri-ously interpreted in any other way. The construction of the temple on the site of the fountain from which the blue and red water flowed is also significant, and shows that the gods ruling over it symbolized the mystic formula of 'burning water.'"[5] It is essential to point out in conjunction with not only "Teotihuacán y 13 de agosto" but with many of Pellicer's poems such as "Uxmal" and *Con palabras y fuego,* that one of the persistent themes in his poetry which links him to the poet Octavio Paz and the novelist Carlos Fuentes is the thesis that Mexico's ritual or mythic past is a viable force in the shaping of twentieth-century realities.

Among the most important symbols in Pellicer's topology of the tropics is the figure of the sun—the dominant image of "Flora solar" ("Solar Flower"). "Flora solar" may well be viewed as the cardinal poem in a long series of poems on or about the sun. From Pellicer's earliest verse in *Colores en el mar y otros poemas,* the sun has been a constant and central image in his poetry.

"Flora solar" is a hymn to solar energy. The poem opens with the figure of the naked poet rising from the water. The presence of the sun is presented as immediate and corporeal: "In each one of my pores, I feel the sun" ("En cada uno de mis poros, el sol" [647]). In the second stanza, an important aquatic image appears as the poet declares: "I am the ancient river of youth" ("Yo soy el viejo río de juventud" [647]). Not only is the figure of the poetic narrator linked to the forces of nature but the sun is variously personified as a leopard and a large woman.

The sun is depicted here as more than the mere decorative, visual image it was in *Colores en el mar.* Here it achieves a ritualistic or mythic importance. The degree of interpenetration between man and nature is such that the poet states in the next to the last stanza: "My brothers the rivers, my brothers the trees/ the birds-the Sun . . ." ("Mis hermanos los ríos, mis hermanos los árboles/ los pájaros-el sol" [649]). As Pabón has noted, the poem records this vital and mystic relationship between Pellicer and the sun, whose transformations the reader perceives continuously throughout the poem.[6] While discussing the importance of the sun images, Carolyn Schlak focuses on the social implications of the poem: "The final stanza of 'Flora Solar' is a plea for brotherhood among men. Here the sun symbolizes man's capacity for the good and the beautiful. Pellicer wants to transmit the sun's primitive innocence to man, thus initiating a reign of peace and love."[7] In spite of the fact that both critics have elected to discuss different aspects of the poem, they are agreed on one point: the figure of the sun in "Flora Solar" is but one link in a long chain of evidence pointing to a special sun symbology in Pellicer's poetry.

II *Religious Poems*

The most significant group of related poems found in his uncollected works are the "Cosillas para el nacimiento" ("Things for the Nativity"). Their importance to the poet is made clear in the following prefatory note:

These little poems justify my life long passion for all which is Christian. I believe in Christ as God and the only important reality in the history of the world. All the rest, art, science, etc. is accessory, secondary, and anecdotal. I have always organized 'The Nativity' each Christmas in my home. I am sure that it is the only important thing that I have ever done. It's almost a masterpiece. I have been able to bring together the art of modeling, music, and poetry every year. Thousands of people come to my home for six or seven weeks . . . to look at the Nativity. The poems which make up this section were always written hours after I finished my yearly work.

My mother, as human as she is religious, started me on the divine practice of 'The Nativity.' Thanks to God and to her I could, I can, do each December that which lasts a month and seems eternal.[8]

There are fifteen poems brought together under this heading. The earliest dated piece is from 1946 and the most recent, 1957. As a whole, they are most reminiscent of a number of the sonnets to the Virgin Mary in *Práctica de vuelo*. The diction is elemental and direct. The majority of the poems are brief descriptions of landscapes. Even while he is describing the landscapes of the Nativity, the ever-present drive to fuse man with nature surfaces. For example, in the ninth poem, the poet addresses the "mystic landscape of stone and sky," declaring:

> With my tropical muscles, I have broken
> the volcanic innocence of your breast
> and with my hands which smell like sunlight
> I have brought you here . . .
> Open your bosom to me, mystic landscape . . .
> so that I may be a part of your body. . . .

> Desde mis músculos tropicales he roto
> la inocencia volcánica de tu pecho
> y con mis manos que huelen a sol
> te he traído aquí . . . ,
> Ábreme tu pecho, místico paisaje,
> para que yo forme parte de tu cuerpo. . . .

(626–27)

The nativity scene thus becomes a microcosm of the universe and the epitome of a larger cosmic unity with which the poet seeks union.

III *Occasional Poetry*

Apart from this group of religious poems, the remaining selections are difficult to classify. There is, however, an amorous-confessional attitude which connects several poems on a thematic plane. For example, the uncollected poems in *Material poético* begin with a poem called "Confesión" ("Confession"). The poem, dated August 23, 1959, echoes the familiar but somewhat minor theme of dissatisfaction with his creative powers. As early as 6, 7 *poems* in "Deseos" ("Desires"), he had lamented the superficiality of his verse. In the opening lines of this poem, he characterizes himself as "inflammable material, eager for light" ("materia inflamable, codicioso de luz" [551]). The poet feels trapped within the confines of his own artistic limitations and wants to break away. He cries "The Quetzal is mute from being so beautiful/ perfect beauty has nothing to say" ("El quetzal está mudo de ser tan hermoso:/ La belleza perfecta nada tiene que decir" [551]).

Love poetry, at least amatory verse, is a rarity in Pellicer. In "Recuerdos" ("Memories"), a group of three poems dated July 13, 1955, Pellicer recalls an absent lover. What makes the poem unique however are its markedly erotic overtones which, with the exception of a few poems in *Hora de junio (Hour of June)*, is unusual in Pellicer. For example, in the third stanza of the first poem the poet affirms:

> I love your naked body,
> like a cloud reflected on water
> I die and am reborn embracing your body.

> Amo tu cuerpo desnudo
> como a una nube reflejada en el agua.
> Muero y renazco estrechando tu cuerpo.
>
> (553)

In the first lines of the third poem, a reference is made to the sonnets of *Hora de junio:*

> Before it was June. Now it's September.
> I think of you and my love is so great,

I think of you and my love is so strong,
that the dazzling light of June
is now the fruitlike nectar of September.

Antes era Junio. Ahora es Septiembre.
Pienso en ti y mi amor es tan grande,
pienso en ti y el amor es tan fuerte
que la luz deslumbrante de Junio
es el jugo frutal de Septiembre.

(555)

"Canto Destruido" ("Song of Ruin") seems related to his other amorous poems. Vaguely reminiscent of some of Neruda's *Residencia* pieces, it is a poem of farewell and melancholy. The poet now lives in a world which is closed, where "time withers, and light turns to dust." It is a world of resignation and acceptance in which the poet's eyes "ache from not crying":

In the ruined bedroom of your absence
trampled twilights bring to life
their tattered clothes, laden with memories. . . .

En la destruida alcoba de tu ausencia
pisoteados crepúsculos reviven
sus harapos, morados de recuerdos. . . .

(557)

There is also in the uncollected poems of Pellicer a great deal of occasional poetry. Among the more notable examples of this tendency are his "Siete sonetos para Gabriela Mistral" ("Seven Sonnets for Gabriela Mistral"), dedicated to Palma Guillén and written in honor of the Nobel Prize laureate from Chile, the three sonnets to Frida Kahlo, the wife of Diego Rivera, and four sonnets to the painter Alberto Gironella. Painters in particular seem to be the object of special attention in Pellicer's verse. Perhaps the most well-known of these poems is his "A Rufino Tamayo" ("To Rufino Tamayo") which continues the colorist tradition of his earliest verse.

Somewhat prophetically, the last poem in the *Material poético* is "He olvidado mi nombre" ("I Have Forgotten my Name"). Among most often-quoted and anthologized poems, "He olvidado mi nombre" is a chronicle of the poet's return to nature. Pellicer records a moment of cosmic splendor when the nameless poet runs naked like a jaguar through the lush tropical underbrush. It is a happy, frenetic world where normal order and relationships are suddenly changed:

> And I, nameless, and with my nameless body
> calling yellow blue and yellow
> that which could never be yellow;
> happy, without a sense of color. . . .
>
> Y yo sin nombre y solo con mi cuerpo sin nombre
> llamándole amarillo al azul y amarillo
> a lo que nunca puede jamás ser amarillo;
> feliz, desconocido de todos los colores. . . .
>
> (651)

The poem culminates a long tradition of myth-oriented poetry in which Pellicer has alluded to an innate longing to be carried away in space and time to a place of primordial tropical origins:

> I feel that a land like Tabasco
> carries me away amid its rivers, searching for forests,
> woods so young that it grieves me to hear them
> spelling out the names of the augur birds.
>
> Siento que un territorio parecido a Tabasco
> me lleva entre sus ríos inaugurando bosques,
> unos bosques tan jóvenes que da pena escucharlos
> deletreando los nombres de los pájaros.
>
> (651)

By placing himself at a distance from the reader, the poet assumes the same posture he had in "Uxmal." The use of the third-person reflexive object pronoun illustrates this technique. The poem begins with the following declaration: "I have forgotten my name./ Anything would be possible but being called Carlos . . ." ("He olvidado mi nombre./ Todo será posible menos llamarse Carlos . . ." [651]).

Through a gradual accretion of sense impressions, Pellicer stresses the physical and tactile aspects of his reverie. It is as if his freed spirit was involved in a process of simultaneous and multiple transformation from tree to jaguar to fish. This is somewhat akin to a process known by mythologists as "complex fusion," a phenomenon through which complex creations are formed by successive linkings

of one element to another. The end result in Pellicer's composition
is not the creation of some multidimensional deity but an ultimate
transformation into a suggestive and all-encompassing image such as
the river:

> The well-bathed river, all naked and strong
> without a name of color or song
> protected from the Sun by the giant Toh leaf
> Anything will be possible but being called Carlos.

> El bien bañado río todo desnudo y fuerte,
> sin nombre de colores ni de cantos.
> Defendido del Sol con la hoja de tóh.
> Todo será posible menos llamarse Carlos.

(652)

CHAPTER 10

Final Appraisal

A passage from Jorge Carrera Andrade's *Reflections on Spanish-American Poetry* illustrates the problems of Pellicer's ambivalent position in the world of both Mexican and Spanish-American letters: "In what we might call Spanish-American geopoetry there is a luminous tropical zone which contrasts with dark or at least misty grey poetry. In this sector of light there are poets such as Carlos Pellicer, Pardo García, Octavio Paz, Nicolás Guillén. 'Tropics why did you give me/ hands full of color? Everything I touch/ will fill with sun,' says Pellicer. His work is marked with a new American vitality, with deep roots in the earth."[1] While on the one hand, it has been his dazzling and sensuous tropicalism which has most attracted critical attention, this same quality has been responsible for critical misinterpretation. In the following pages, drawing upon our previous comments on his verse, we will attempt to describe Pellicer's significance to literature and in so doing attempt to place the figure of this poet in a more balanced and realistic perspective.

I The Originality of the Artist

In terms of literary groups and movements, it is difficult to relate the poetic works of Pellicer to other important figures of his time in Mexico. He cannot easily be related to the writers of the *Contemporáneos* generation, for theirs was a poetry of revolt in the tradition of the European vanguard. His was a poetry of rebellion within a unique social-mythic context. As the poet-critic Octavio Paz has suggested, Pellicer is the first truly modern poet in Mexico. The following comments, which appeared as a prefatory note to Pellicer's verse in the anthology, *Poesía en movimiento (Poetry in Motion)*, form a most suggestive critical formulation on him:

If López Velarde and Tablada begin our contemporary poetry, Carlos Pellicer is the first really modern poet in Mexico. He doesn't react against

141

modernism: he incorporates it into vanguardism, taking from this and other literary movements what he needs to say and what he wants to say. When many of the contemporaries were exploring the subconscious, Pellicer rediscovered the beauty of the world: the sun which shines over the lush tropical rivers, the sea . . . His words want to reorder creation. And in the "loving tropics" the elements fuse together: land, air, water, and fire let him see "in living flesh the beauty of God." Magical and in continuous metamorphosis, his poetry is neither reasoning nor sermonizing, but rather song.[2]

Paz' emphasis on the magic or telluric aspects of Pellicer's poetry are related tangentially to the comments of the critic Carlos Monsiváis which appeared in the well-known anthology, *La poesía mexicana del siglo XX (Twentieth-century Mexican Poetry)*. Monsivais relates Pellicer to a broader context of Latin American regional literature: ". . . he belongs, spiritually, to that generation, which guided by the inspiration of José Eustasio Rivera was dedicated to the discovery of Latin America, animated and moved by a tropical instinct."[3] The remarks of Paz and Monsiváis point to a number of directions in which Pellicer's poetry seems to move: inward toward a reaffirmation of the cultural values of the Mexican man and outward in the direction of a continental or universal vision of the tropics. With reference to this first category, we have seen that Pellicer was unique among the poets of his generation in his quest to rediscover and reaffirm his indigenous heritage.

One of the most singular features of his poetry in the context of contemporary Mexican letters is its function in the interpretation of pre-Columbian myth. The ideas of Northrop Frye on the relationship between myth and poetry may be helpful at this point. He writes: "When poets re-create myth, they work in a different direction from the conceptual tendencies of the allegorists. The poet's impulse is to retell the story, or invent a new one with the same characters, instead of rationalizing the story. His cultural influence is thus in stressing the concrete, personal, story-telling elements in the myth which the conceptualizers tend to pass over or treat as archaic."[4]

We have seen how Pellicer's mythic faculties work on precisely this plane. The expanded "Oda a Cuauhtémoc" is a case in point, for here myth, legend, and historic circumstance have been fused together, reenacted by Pellicer, in a poetic response to a social reality—the problems associated with the emergence of modern

Mexico. We have seen repeated instances in which the artistic motifs of the pre-Hispanic world, the quincunx, the four elements, the jaguar, the image of burning water, appeared as central elements in his verse. Used singly or in combination in such poems as "Esquemas para una oda tropical," "Uxmal," "El canto del Usumacinta," and "Teotihuacán y 13 de agosto," these motifs evoke a portrait of the universe in which man is depicted as a vital link in a process of creation which stems from the union of opposing forces. This may help explain the significance of the man-tree image which occurs with such regularity in Pellicer's poetry. In addition to noting the appearance of these motifs it is important to stress their impact on the structure and design of a number of individual poems.

If we are to attempt to characterize Pellicer's art in general terms it might be useful to point out that in many of his important poems which are based on mythological allusion ("Uxmal," "Esquemas para una oda tropical," "El canto del Usumacinta," "Surgente fin," and "Teotihuacán") the poetic narrator assumes the stance of a high priest or soothsayer, thus objectifying after a fashion, the narration of the myth. This may take the form of an implicit hallucination (as in "Uxmal") or a slow drifting to sleep (as in "Surgente fin"). What is important to note, however, is that the mythic aspects of Pellicer's work are cast into a carefully wrought and aesthetically valid framework. It is also apparent that much of the mythic material in Pellicer's works is derived from specific sources. For example, the "Romance de Tilantongo" can be traced to the Mixteca legend of creation found in Father Burgoa's *Historia de Oaxaca (History of Oaxaca)*, whereas the allusion to the metamorphosis of Quetzalcoatl into Venus in "Teotihuacán" is a broad-based legend in Nahua-Aztec culture.

In lieu of repeating what we have already said about Pellicer's debt to pre-Columbian ritual myth, it might be more meaningful to select one symbol, the pyramid, to show how its use places Pellicer in the mainstream of contemporary Mexican letters. The figure of the pyramid is evoked on at least three occasions in Pellicer's verse: in "Uxmal" where it appears as an imposing ritual allusion ("a platform gigantic"); in "Esquemas para una oda tropical" where it is a symbol of fusion and creation ("the culminating center/ of my life's truncated pyramid") and in "Teotihuacán y 13 de agosto" where it is presented as a more complex representation of the whole structure of the pre-Columbian cosmos. It is worth noting that the pyramid as

a symbol of pre-Hispanic civilization has been evoked frequently in
contemporary Mexican literature, notably by Octavio Paz and Carlos Fuentes. In two works in particular by these authors, *Posdata*
(Postscript) by Paz and *Todos los gatos son pardos (All the Cats are*
Brown) by Fuentes, the symbol of the pyramid is used in a sugges-
tively similar fashion.[5] This discussion serves to highlight one very
important aspect in the work of Pellicer and such younger writers as
Paz and Fuentes: the emphasis that all three place on the underly-
ing and vital influence of pre-Columbian cosmologies on the Mexico
of today.

Apart from these general observations, there are specific linguistic and stylistic innovations in Pellicer's poetry which signal his
important role as a transitional figure in twentieth-century Mexican
letters. The use of specific images and sense impressions by Pellicer
(namely the sun, the sea, and various vegetable-animal figures) call
attention to the relationship between Pellicer and the entire corpus
of postrevolutionary literature including the Indianist novel and the
novel of the land. One of the most obvious and recurrent features of
Pellicer's poetic diction is the intensity and frequency with which he
depicts aspects of the natural world linked to man. The process
which Dauster calls "intermixture," Gamboa "consubstantiation,"
and Schlak, "materialization," all refer (tangentially at least) to some
form of identification of human beings with plants and animals. We
have already seen how the use of particularly the sun and man-tree
images may be clarified in terms of the pre-Columbian symbologies
to which Pellicer seems so indebted. Even if one were to ignore
these implications, the tropes themselves evoke impressive visual
images which are virtually self-explanatory and aesthetically valid as
natural symbols of interpenetration or fusion.

II *Pellicer in Spanish America*

While Pellicer's passion for the pre-Hispanic and the essentially
Mexican, has earned him a special place in his own national literature, his influence and importance clearly transcend national
boundaries.

In his *Esquema generacional de las letras hispanoamericanas*
(Generational Outline of Spanish-American Letters), José Juan
Arrom groups Pellicer with a constellation of poets born between
1894 and 1924 and called the "Generation of 1924." Among these,
namely Nicolás Guillén, Pablo Neruda, and Jorge Carrera Andrade,

there are several who in their own way parallel the career of Pellicer. They were all born within six years of one another. Pellicer is the oldest, Neruda and Guillén were born in 1904, and Carrera Andrade in 1903. More importantly, they share a common mythic vision of Latin American reality.

The affinities between Guillén and Pellicer are clear-cut and immediate. The two, who met during the Spanish Civil War, are most often associated because of their so-called overt tropicalism, but the relationship points to a deeper and more fundamental set of attitudes rooted in their common denunciation of racial and social injustice. In Pellicer's *Piedra de sacrificios,* there are strong denunciations of United States' exploitation in the Caribbean and Mexico as well as a plea for Latin American unity. In poems such as "Divagación del puerto" ("Port Digression"), "Elegía" ("Elegy"), "Historia" ("History"), "Cuba divina" ("Divine Cuba"), and "Balada trágica del corazón" ("The Tragic Ballad of the Heart"), his disillusionment over Anglo-American economic imperialism led to a series of bitter caricatures of the American presence in the Caribbean and often included the reproduction of crass sounding commercial slogans and phrases. Pellicer gradually moved away from this overt social criticism, and in works such as *Con palabras y fuego,* introduced archetypal figures of redemption who would salvage whole nations of oppressed peoples. Thematically and technically, Pellicer and Guillén show a number of parallels. Thus while Guillén began by exploiting the rhythmic and onomotopoeic possibilities of the *son,* a Cuban song-dance form, in *Motivos del son (Son Motifs,* 1930), he shifts direction in *Sóngoro cosongo* (1931) and *West Indies Ltd.* (1934) and focuses on the dismal economic conditions of the Cuban blacks. In "Caña" ("Cane"), for example he epigrammatically contrasted the "haves" and the "have-nots":

> Black man
> in the cane fields
> yankee
> above the cane fields. . . .

> El negro
> junto al cañaveral
> El yanqui
> sobre el cañaveral.[6]

Apart from this superficial, declamatory propensity, Pellicer and Guillén are linked on a more significant level. This is their mutual tendency to examine the racial heritage of their peoples. And we are not referring here to mere race alone but to a timeless tradition which harkens back to a primordial tropical beginning. For example, Guillén's "Llegada" ("Arrival") parallels poems such as Pellicer's "Oda a Cuauhtémoc" and "13 de agosto: Ruina de Tenochtitlán" where clusters of telluric images (sun, rain, tropical fauna) become connecting elements in the story of man's creation. While Pellicer focuses on the glories of the indigenous civilizations of the Americas, Guillén directs his attention to the black man of Africa:

> Here we are!
> The word comes to us moist from the forest,
> and a vital sun rises in our veins.
> Our fist is strong,
> sustains the oar.
>
> Exorbitant palms sleep in the deep eye.
> The shout escapes us like a drop of pure gold.[7]
>
> ¡Aquí estamos!
> La palabra nos viene húmeda de los bosques,
> y un sol enérgico nos amanece entre las venas.
> El puño es fuerte
> y tiene el remo.
>
> En el ojo profundo duermen palmeras exorbitantes.
> El grito se nos sale como una gota de oro virgen.

Another striking example of their similar tendency to explore an unrecorded past is Pellicer's "He olvidado mi nombre" ("I Have Forgotten my Name") and Guillén's "Elapellido" ("My Last Name"). Just as Pellicer's poem is a journey back to primordial origins, Guillén's composition centers about a nebulous voyage to the author's ancestral beginnings:

> Are you sure it is my name?
> Have you got all my particulars?
> Do you already know my navigable blood,
> my geography full of dark mountains,
> of deep and bitter valleys
> that are not on the maps?[8]

¿Es mi nombre, estáis ciertos?
¿Tenéis todas mis señas?
¿Ya conocéis mi sangre navegable,
mi geografía llena de oscuros montes,
de hondos y amargos valles
que no están en los mapas?

There is the question, too, of the poets' tropicalism. Both Pellicer and Guillén wrote eulogies of the great tropical cities Río, Havana, and São Paulo, as well as an apostrophe to the tropics incarnate. The opening lines of Guillén's "Palabras en el trópico" ("Words in the Tropics") call to mind the poets' stylistic affinities:

Tropics,
with your bright flames
toasting the high clouds. . . .
You pierce
with a great red arrow
the heart of the jungles
and the flesh of the rivers!

Trópico,
tu clara hoguera
tuesta las nubes altas. . . .
Tú atraviesas
con una gran flecha roja
el corazón de las selvas
y la carne de los ríos.

There also exist inherent structural and stylistic differences between the two poets, so there is danger in going too far in a comparison of a limited number of external factors. However, in general terms, the careers of the two men offer surprising parallels. They both began their writing under the influence of the wanning modernist wave, each moving away to cultivate a highly personal form of verse distinct from the literary mode of the day. As Pellicer drifted away from the group of avant-garde writers known as the *Contemporáneos,* so did Guillén divorce himself from the reigning intellectual elite of Havana known as the *grupo minorista* ("the minority group") who were clustered around the literary review *Revista de Avance (The Advance Journal).* The thematic progress of their poetry is also similar, each moving from themes of national concern in their early works to ones of more universal scope in their later verse. Most importantly, their voices are directed toward the same collective consciousness of the underdeveloped or Third World nations.

Although a comparison between Pellicer and the Nobel laureate Pablo Neruda yields less clear-cut and specific analogies, it is nonetheless helpful in appreciating the relationship between Pellicer and the most well-known of his contemporaries. Like Pellicer, Neruda was a professional writer and world traveler, but the technique and texture of much of his poetry is quite different from that of Pellicer. While Pellicer's early works are characterized by lyric simplicity and colorist excess, Neruda's first important collections, *Residencia en la tierra I & II (Residence on Earth I & II)* published in 1933 and 1935, are journeys into the world of the surreal. They describe, in the words of the critic Luis Monguió, "a world of aches and powdery glances, of paper and brooms, pallid days, decrepit objects, graveyards and tailor shops, and orthopedic appliances."[9]

They appear diametrically opposed to the bright world of azure skies and tropical suns painted by Pellicer at the same moment. However, initially with the publication of *Canto general (General Song)* and his works that followed, Neruda moves to a poetry of social communion and political cause. We see the same anti-American epithets of Pellicer's early period cast in a different poet mold:

> When the trumpets had sounded and all
> was in readiness on the face of the earth,
> Jehovah divided his universe:
> Anaconda, Ford Motors,
> Coca-Cola Inc., and similar entities:
> the most succulent item of all,
> The United Fruit Company Incorporated
> reserved for itself: the heartland
> and coasts of my country. . . .[10]

> Cuando sonó la trompeta, estuvo
> todo preparado en la tierra,
> y Jehová repartió el mundo
> a Coca-Cola Inc., Anaconda,
> Ford Motors, y otras entidades:

> la Compañía Frutera Inc.
> se reservó lo más jugoso,
> la costa central de mi tierra.

It would be a superficial judgment to compare Pellicer and Neruda on the basis of their anti-American writings alone, since such poetry is commonplace in Spanish America. What links them on a more profound and substantial level, however, is their cosmogonic world view. As Monguió alerts the reader of Neruda: "In *Canto general* it is water and earth, the air and the primordial slime, self-spawned and begetting beasts, vegetation, and men of America, that he celebrates, above all."[11] More ambitious in scope than *Con palabras y fuego (With Words and Fire)*, *Canto general* chronicles the new world from the days of pre-Columbian splendor through the Discovery and Conquest to the present. Here, as in later collections, is where his relationship to Pellicer becomes more evident. For example, in "América, no invoco tu nombre en vano" ("America, I do not call your name without hope") he stresses his symbiotic relationship with the American continent:

> I live in the darkness which makes me what I am,
> I sleep and awake in your fundamental sunrise:
> as mild as the grapes, and as terrible,
> carrier of sugar and the whip,
> soaked in the sperm of your species,
> nursed on the blood of your inheritance.[12]

> Vivo en la sombra que me determina,
> duermo y despierto en tu esencial aurora:
> dulce como las uvas, y terrible,
> conductor del azúcar y el castigo,
> empapado en esperma de tu especie,
> amamantado en sangre de tu herencia.

Not only do Pellicer and Neruda celebrate the creation of the poetic universe and sing songs in praise of America, but theirs is a poetry of discovery and a cataloging of the vast landscapes and exotic flora and fauna of the Americas. In an interview, Neruda spoke of the tradition of landscape poetry in Latin America: "I would say to the young poets of my country and of Latin America—perhaps this is our tradition—to discover things, to be in the sea, to be in the moun-

tains, and approach every living thing. And how can you not love
such an approach to life, that has such extravagant surprises?"[13]

It is this same sense of discovery, this yearning to describe the
physical wonder of the Latin American landscape, which links Pellicer to another Latin American poet of the twentieth century, the
Ecuatorian Jorge Carrera Andrade. In his recent book, *Reflections
on Spanish-American Poetry*, Carrera Andrade summarized the cy-
cles through which his art has passed: "There was the path of a
poetry of things, there was the poetry of travel and discovery, the
one of social revolt, and finally that of a planetary Utopia."[14] In
many ways, this outline parallels the progress of Pellicer's verse
beginning with an obsession to deal with the sensations and colors of
his native tropics, followed by a number of travel poems, and finally
reaching a new plateau of maturity in a series of myth-oriented
interpretations of the cosmos. But what solidly links the poets is not
so much the similarity of their careers but the texture of their
poetry. Theirs is a poetry of "things." Objects, animate or inanimate, are strung together to create great verbal tapestries of the
tropics. The British Hispanist G. R. Coulthard described the work
of Carrera Andrade as having: "one vital theme: a delectation in the
physical sensations of the world, a delight in things. . . . These early
poems are made up of acute observations of objects and living
beings—their shapes, colors, their visual and tactile reality. . . ."[15]
Thus like Pellicer, Carrera Andrade is a poet of tropical luxuriance.
He celebrates in his poems the affinities between man and nature.
His "La llave de fuego" ("The Key of Fire") with its interlacing
fluvial and vegetable images calls to mind Pellicer's "Esquemas para
una oda tropical":

> The maize smiles at me and speaks between its teeth
> a language of water and dew,
> the schoolmaster maize which teaches
> the birds to count on its abacus.
> I speak with the maize and the guacamayo
> that know the history of the flood
> the memory of which, clouds the brow of the rivers.
> The rivers run on, forward, ever forward. . . .[16]

> Me sonríe el maíz y habla entre dientes
> un lenguaje de agua y de rocío,

el maíz pedagógico que enseña
a contar a los pájaros en su ábaco.
Yo hablo con el maíz y el guacamayo
que conocen la historia del diluvio
cuyo recuerdo nubla la frente de los ríos.
Los ríos adelante corren, siempre adelante.

III   *A Final Glance*

Pellicer's celebration of the physical and cosmic splendors of the New World, his constant identification with the immediate world of the senses, and pervasive concern for social justice, clearly place him in the mainstream of twentieth-century Spanish-American literature. Thus he is a unique figure in Mexican literature serving as a link between European vanguardism and the tradition of social realism inspired by the Mexican Revolution, and on a more universal scale, a representative of Latin America's poetry of the Third World.

At the beginning of this book we raised the question of Pellicer's ambivalent position in the world of Spanish-American letters. While he has received strong critical acclaim both in Mexico and abroad, he is perhaps the least-known writer of his generation. This may be due in part to a repetition of early critical labels, a tendency to stereotype him as an exclusively visual poet. It is also apparent that of the poets of the *Contemporáneos* generation he is the least European, culturally and stylistically the farthest away from the world of Anglo-American letters, and the most difficult to capture in translation. Pellicer's poems are great concerts of light and movement, at once visual and sensuous and paradoxically evasive to capture and define. Robert Bly's comments on César Vallejo seem to apply for many of Pellicer's poems are "like flashes of light in a room already light."[17] While some of his poems are lineal, almost facile, others are difficult even for those who read poetry a great deal. Then, too, there is the problem of Pellicer's commitment to social causes which surfaces with regularity in his verse. As Carrera Andrade points out, citing the critic Malcolm Cowley, poetry in England and the United States does not try to perform a social function whereas the poet in Spanish America considers himself the voice of a collective "I." Pellicer's passionate dedication to his art epitomizes the finest in this long tradition of poetry of involvement in Spanish America. He has seen and recorded with intense subjectivity both the physical and spiritual dimensions of the New World. As he has matured his poetry has evolved from strident outcry to muted song.

Pellicer summarized his ideas on the relationship of art to society in an interview with this writer on June 5, 1972. His own comments are a fitting conclusion to this study:

I think that the poetic approach between peoples is very important. Poetry is a whole testimony of art. Poetry is music; it is painting; it is sculpture, and it is not made with words alone. I find it in Christianity. I always place Christianity above all things. Christianity is a message of love difficult to realize because all of Christianity is based on the principle of pardon and the most difficult thing for a human being to do is to pardon. Thus we see that Christianity has not had until today the true importance that it will have some day. Wells, in his summary of universal history, defines Christianity very well and says that it is an alarming doctrine. He is right. He is right because we do not exercise it. And without pardon there is no love. Well, yes, I have admiration for Marx, who does not have? But before Marx comes the Christian message. In Marx is all that enormous wisdom about the economy. Probably he thought that when the goods of the earth would be more or less divided up there would be an atmosphere of cordiality in the entire world. Christianity goes ahead; it goes with love. But this involves not only refraining from egoism, but sharing what one has with others, not being selfish and knowing how to pardon. This, for me, is the great secret and the really great newness of the Christian message. . . .

Notes and References

Preface

1. For a discussion of critical reactions to Pellicer, see the author's article, "The Critics and Carlos Pellicer," *The University of South Florida Language Quarterly* 11 (Fall–Winter 1972), 39–41.

2. ". . . ha sido reconocido unánimamente como el más grande poeta mexicano contemporáneo," *Imagen de la poesía mexicana contemporánea* (Mexico City, 1959), p. 91.

3. "Carlos Pellicer . . . es actualmente, si no el mejor, uno de los más grandes poetas que ha dado la tierra mexicana," *Sur* 272 (September–October, 1961), 27.

4. "Pellicer es el más rico y vasto de los poetas de su generación," *Las peras del olmo* (Barcelona, 1971), p. 82.

Chapter One

1. Quoted in Carlos González Peña, *History of Mexican Literature*, trans. G. B. Nance and F. J. Dunstan (Dallas, 1968), p. 264.

2. Arturo Torres Ríoseco, *New World Literature* (Berkeley, 1959), p. 187.

3. *In Quest of Identity: Patterns in the Spanish American Essay of Ideas, 1890–1960* (Chapel Hill, 1967), p. 47.

4. ". . . sería injusto no reconocer lo que sirvió—a los más jóvenes—el ejemplo de probidad intelectual de González Martínez, la lección de energía de José Vasconcelos y la sutil curiosidad de Alfonso Reyes. Más que su influencia directa, lo que recibimos, a través de ellos, fue el mensaje del mundo literario y filosófico, en que iban plasmando sus propias conquistas," "Perspectiva de la literatura mexicana actual" *(Contemporáneos* 2, no. 4 [1928], 23).

5. "el dios mayor y casi único de nuestra poesía" *(La poesía de los jóvenes de México* [Mexico City, 1924], p. 12).

6. "La inteligencia de Antonio Caso resplandecía mejor, sin duda, a la luz escolar de la cátedra, pero el talento y la sensibilidad de González Martínez se entregaban todos en la conversación" *(Contemporáneos* 2, no. 4 [1928], 7).

7. *Xavier Villaurrutia* (New York, 1971), p. 16.

8. "Estas dos influencias, tan opuestas, se combinaron en la obra de todos o casi todos los neuvos. Del uno heredaron el amor a una forma depurada, a un idioma justo, a un pudor intelectual muy severo. Del otro, la curiosidad de nuevas sensaciones, el deseo de una metáfora más original y plástica, el sentido del color y la voluptuosidad del tacto" *(Contemporáneos* 2, no. 4 [1928], 10).

9. "Mis amigos nacieron, o se educaron, en el altiplano. Aun cuando la mayor parte de mi vida la he pasado en el Valle de México, no hay que olvidar que la infancia pesa mucho. Las cosas que me ocurrieron en Tabasco durante la niñez (la muerte de mi hermano Ernesto, mi primer viaje al mar, el amor a mi madre) son impresiones y emociones que fueron carburando, lentamente, en lo que más tarde hice o actué con el idioma. Todas esas cosas siguen pesando en mi vida. Yo he sido un tropical insobornable" (quoted in Emmanuel Carballo, *Diecinueve protagonistas de la literatura mexicana del siglo XX* [Mexico City, 1965], p. 194).

10. "Como sus poemas, lo primero que su persona se manifestaba eran los adjetivos: la corbata de seda espesa, los calcetines brillantes; y en el meñique, un espléndido solitario" *(Tiempo de arena,* in *Obras escogidas de Jaime Torres Bodet* [Mexico City, 1961], p. 232).

11. "Hoja de combate, iconoclasta, causó más de un disgusto en el cuerpo de profesores" (Mario Puga, "Carlos Pellicer," *Universidad de México* 10 [February, 1956], 17).

12. "Este grupo en el cual—figuraban Carlos Pellicer, Martín Gómez Palacio, Bernardo Ortiz de Montellano, José Gorostiza y Enrique González Rojo, se encontraba concebido dentro de tal elasticidad que pudo subsistir sin oponerse a la libertad individual de cada uno de sus miembros" *(Contemporáneos* 2, no. 4 [1928], 28).

13. "Esta revista no es portavoz de un grupo—ni literario ni político . . . se halla dispuesta a reconocer todos los valores intelectuales, sin aceptar o rechazar ciegamente los consagrados o los desconocidos" (quoted in Merlin H. Forster, *An Index to Mexican Literary Periodicals* [New York, 1966], p. 9).

14. "Pero es honrado declarar que *Ulises* no representa de ninguna manera el 'sentir nacional' " (Forster, *An Index,* p. 17).

15. For a description of the journal see Boyd G. Carter, *Historia de la literatura hispanoamericana a través de sus revistas* (Mexico, 1968), pp. 105–7, and B. G. Carter, *Las revistas literarias de Hispanoamérica* (Mexico City, 1959), pp. 98–99. The latter contains an extensive bibliography on other vanguard reviews (pp. 109–11) and on vanguardism in general (pp. 246–51). The importance of *Contemporáneos* in Mexican literature is discussed in this author's article, *"The Revista Contemporáneos:* A New Dimension in Contemporary Mexican Literature," *University of South Florida Language Quarterly* 7 (Fall–Winter, 1969), 27–32.

16. *Contemporáneos*, 4, no. 18 (1929), 335–336.

17. *Contemporáneos*, 5, no. 23 (1930), 77–81.

18. *Contemporáneos*, 7, no. 37 (1931), 195–200.

19. "El buen arte es individual y no debe mezclársele con los movimientos sociales colectivos, por obligación y previsión." *(Contemporáneos*, 4, no. 18 [1929], 336).

20. "El arte no es revolucionario porque hable de o exhiba los fenómenos materiales de la revolución, es revolucionario por sí y en sí mismo. (¿Qué en el Renacimiento el tema cristiano define la calidad artística de los pintores?)" *(Contemporáneos*, 4, no. 18 [1929], 336).

21. "Lo que logró hacer la revolución mexicana con la nueva generación de escritores, puestos desde la infancia a comprobar la amarga realidad de esa revolución, fue convencerlos de la existencia de una sensibilidad personal, mientras más personal más genuinamente mexicana, en donde había que ahondar sin retrasarse con la cultura del mundo." *(Contemporáneos*, 5 no. 23, [1930], 80).

22. "Como señalamos, a propósito de la poesía de López Velarde, los beneficios, la influencia de la revolución mexicana en el arte debemos buscarla, más que en los frutos inmediatos que arrancan del árbol de los hechos nuestros novelistas, en la semilla que un nuevo sentido de los valores espirituales, con vistas al tono verdadero de la sensibilidad mexicana, a la cultura y a las ideas universales, puedan aportar sus obras." *(Contemporáneos*, 7, no. 37 [1931], 200).

23. "todos estos escritores que viven conscientemente la vida de su país—sus problemas, su tradición, su sensibilidad—tienen que reflejarla en formas universales, primera condición de la cultura y aspiración del hombre moderno." *(Contemporáneos*, 7, no. 37 [1931], 210).

24. Desde luego elogiamos la actitud de los redactores de *Crisol*, convertidos a tiempo hacia el estudio de los problemas revolucionarios, porque pensamos que a la Revolución mexicana antes que una literatura vana o sustantiva le falta el estudio verdadero y profundo de sus fines. *Crisol* tiene la obligación, de acuerdo con sus propósitos, de fijar con profundidad y sabiduría el ideal revolucionario, *único* cuidando de caer en la política inmediata." *(Contemporáneos*, 4, no. 18, [1929], 333).

25. "Se ha acusado a nuestra literatura de esta separación deliberada—¿deliberada?—de sus temas con los que la vida del país le ofrece. . . . Algunos han creído advertir en este decoro de los nuevos artistas de México, un retorno a las doctrinas del arte por el arte. No contentos con advertirlo, han creído que revelarles su aparente descubrimiento era ya acusarlos de desorientación, sin comprender que la más deplorable desorientación era la suya y que la belleza sirvió raras veces para arma política sin perder algo de su adusta perfección." *(Contemporáneos*, 2, no. 4 [1928], 3).

26. "Edifiquemos con estos valores—en el presente—el estilo de una

nueva sensibilidad ética y abandonemos el absurdo de descubrir en las ruinas de una realidad que fue." *(Contemporáneos,* 1, no. 1 [1928], 2*)*.

27. "Los frescos de Diego Rivera, por boca de los personajes representados, cuentan, cantan, maldicen, sobrecogen el ánimo—intentan sobrecogerlo al menos,—con violencias y asperezas, procuran llevar al espectador a un terreno ajeno del que corresponde a un perfecto valor estético, hacen del arte un instrumento político-social, un instrumento mecanizado, mecanizador, poco refinado, y en ese aparte peligroso que hace el camino del artista, ciertas virtudes iniciales se hacen borrosas, se abandonan a la desesperanza deshechas por la narración, la oratoria y la ironía gesticulante." *(Contemporáneos,* 1, no. 1 [1928], 64–65*)*.

28. "Por mi parte, no titubeo en decir que prefiero *La malhora* . . . penúltimo de los libros publicados por Mariano Azuela." *(Contemporáneos,* 5, no. 23 [1930], 79*)*.

29. "Para Pellicer la poesía ha sido el viaje alrededor del mundo en vez del viaje alrededor de nuestra alcoba que la poesía ha sido, hasta ahora, para nosotros . . ." ("Cartas a Olivier," *Ulises,* no. 2 [June, 1927], 14).

30. "Los 'Contemporáneos' siguen atentos al desarrollo poético de este 'extemporáneo' Pellicer, el poeta viajero; algunos admiran aparentemente su poesía , sí pero también puedan atacarlo duramente, en todo aquello que hace de Pellicer un poeta diferente . . . pero es inútil buscar en sus versos otra tendencia que no sea, exclusivamente la del goce completo de los sentidos" *(Antología de la poesía mexicana moderna* [Mexico, 1928], p. 141*)*.

31. "Conservador de los instrumentos musicales de la poesía, ajeno a Góngora, Mallarmé, Valéry, recrea el gozo de las palabras por cuanto deben sonar a los oídos en un sentido paralelo a lo que en la música moderna realizan los nuevos ritmos del jazz" ("Un camino de poesía," *Contemporáneos,* 4, no. 16 [1929], 151).

32. "La música y el color eran las cualidades de esos poemas. Las metáforas se despegaban, a veces, del fondo de la composición; en ocasiones, la unidad del asunto pasaba a segundo término. . . . Pero ¡cuántas plásticas sugestiones contenían aquellos alejandrinos!" *(Tiempo de arena,* p. 232*)*.

33. Edna Worthley Underwood, ed. and trans., *Anthology of Mexican Poets from the Earliest Times to the Present* (Portland, Maine, 1932), p. 48.

34. *Cited in Three Spanish American Poets: Pellicer, Neruda, Andrade,* ed. and trans. Lloyd Mallan et al. (Albuquerque, 1942), p. 4.

35. ". . . la poesía de Pellicer no es tan periférica—carente de profundidad—como se ha dado en decir" ("Carlos Pellicer y el contorno de la Poesía," *América,* no. 36 [April, 1944], 30).

36. Carlos González Salas, "La poesía mexicana actual," *Cuadernos Hispanoamericanos,* no. 104 (August, 1958), 222–31.

37. "Por eso nos parece poco justo que se le siga motejando de poeta

paisajista. Para él, poesía significa compenetración de hombre con naturaleza" ("Aspectos del paisaje en la poesía de Carlos Pellicer," in *Ensayos sobre poesía mexicana* [Mexico City, 1963], p. 47).

38. "Poetry from Mexico." *Times Literary Supplement,* March 29, 1963, p. 218.

39. *Carlos Pellicer: Primera antología poética* (Mexico: Fondo de Cultura Económica, 1969); Pedro Frank de Andrea and George Melynkovich, "Carlos Pellicer: aportación bibliográfica," *Boletín de la Comunidad Latinoamericana de Escritores,* 4 (June, 1969), 8–26.

40. "En la franja de Universo donde la bondad de los Dioses hizo nacer el más divino de los hombres, Simón Bolívar, Libertador de América, la traición y el asesinato infaman esa franja de Universo que se llama Venezuela" (quoted in Pedro F. De Andrea and George Melnykovich, "Carlos Pellicer: Aportación bibliográfica, *Boletín de La Comunidad Latinoamericana de Escritores* 4 [June, 1969], 11).

41. "Traía consigo todo el sol de su tierra andaluza. . . . La visión fugaz del gran cantor gitano permanece en mi memoria. Supe después, por Salvador Novo, que Federico le había hablado con entusiasmo de unos poemas de *Las palomas*" (Mario Puga, "Carlos Pellicer," *Revista Universidad de México* 10 [February, 1956], 19).

Chapter Two

1. "Para mí no tiene sentido alguno la poesía que es puro juego exterior o encanto de los sentidos. La musicalidad de una estrofa, la belleza de ciertas palabras, no me llama en lo absoluto cuando se busca como intención de la poesía" (quoted in F. N. Dauster, *Xavier Villaurrutia* [New York, 1971], p. 31).

2. "El impulso es tan fuerte que las palabras, aun cuando no queden ubicadas con precisión, actúan como si yo estuviera dentro de ellas. Por eso mismo son tan desordenadas, porque yo soy el desorden" (*Diecinueve protagonistas de la literatura mexicana del siglo XX* [Mexico City, 1965], p. 195).

3. Carlos Pellicer, *Material poético* (Mexico: Universidad Nacional Autónoma, 1962), p. 131. All future references to the poetry of Pellicer published prior to 1961 will be to this edition with the page numbers in the text.

4. "El Mar—que no es un aspecto físico del Mundo, sino una manera espiritual—, tiene en mi corazón los elementos principales para subordinarme aé. Por e afán dinámico que predomina en mí, el gran lugar donde se mueve el agua me atrajo soberanamente. . . . Playas de México, playas de Colombia, de Venezuela—repúblicas inolvidables a donde llevé durante dos años la representación de los estudiantes mexicanos—, playas de Cuba, sonoras playas del Atlántico, soberbias playas del Pacífico. La sal y el viento de sus panoramas han invadido mi sangre tornasolándola con todos recuerdos" (*Material poético* [Mexico City, 1962], p. 11).

5. "Mi afinidad con los pintores es inmediata. Siempre he creído que la música es la expresión más importante de la poesía. Vienen después, en orden decreciente, la pintura y la palabra. Si admito que el color y la línea están más cerca de lo que escribo que la palabra, es fácil comprender por que he vivido más próximo a los pintores que a los escritores" *(Diecinueve protagonistas,* pp. 193–94).

6. "Tres aguafuertes sobre la tempestad en los Andes. . . . Sobre esas montañas pasó y triunfó Bolívar en 1819 el más generoso de los hombres y el más grande de los héroes" *(Material poético,* p. 47).

7. Translated by Donald Justice, in *New Mexican Poetry* (New York, 1970), p. 170.

8. "Además de la presentación externa, *Colores en el mar* debe haber causado una de las fáciles tempestades como lo son las del vaso literario, por el contenido. Por lo pronto, hay en él el verso más breve que recuerdo en la poesía mexicana que, por la condensación y la densidad del material poético vence al *hai-kai,* aunque éste además de la brevedad obedezca a otros propósitos. El poema de Pellicer consta de un solo verso: 'Tu belleza y el mar buscan mi estrella'" (El primer libro poético de Carlos Pellicer, *Boletín Bibliográfico,* no. 490 [October, 1973], 15–17).

9. "El asombro ingenuo del poeta y su alegría de tonalidades infantiles se traducen, frente a frente con el lenguaje, en un difícil juego métrico. . . . El complicado juego con el lenguaje atrae al dinamismo infantil que actúa dentro del poeta, porque ofrece múltiples posibilidades de asombros renovados, de inusitados hallazgos" *("El Material poético* de Carlos Pellicer," *Cuadernos Americanos* 124 [September–October, 1962], 239–70).

10. William J. Straub, "Conversation with Jorge Carrera Andrade," *Latin American Literary Review* 1 (Fall, 1972), 73.

11. George Melnykovich, "Carlos Pellicer and Creationism," *Latin American Literary Review* 2 (Spring–Summer, 1974), 102.

12. Ibid, p. 111.

Chapter Three

1. "Pertenece Carlos Pellicer a la nueva familia internacional que tiene por partria el Continente y por estirpe la gente toda de habla española . . . La familia internacional existe y ya sólo le falta hacer prosélitos para dejar de ser una secta y convertirse en un pueblo" *(Material poético,* p. 59).

2. "Desde la nave aérea ha visto Pellicer su América y también la ha escudriñado con la planta del pie que descubre todos los secretos de la tierra y con la mente que contempla la historia. De esta suerte integral ha cultivado su amor del continente latino. Un amor total y sin reservas, como el de la madre que ama a sus hijos. . . . Leyendo estos versos he pensado en una religión nueva que alguna vez soñé predicar: la religión del paisaje; la devoción de la belleza exterior, limpia y grandiosa, sin interpretaciones y sin deformaciones; como lenguaje directo de la gracia divina" (Ibid, p. 59).

3. "Hermanos de la gran familia internacional iberoamericana, acoged este libro de uno de los vuestros, guardadlo con amor, porque contiene palpitaciones de todos los ritmos de neustra patria continental" (Ibid., p. 60).

4. "Literature and Myth," in *Relations of Literacy Study,* ed. James Thorpe (New York, 1967), p. 40.

5. Francisco Pabón, "Gravitación de lo indígena en la poesía de Carlos Pellicer" (Ph. D. diss., Rutgers University, 1969), p. 64.

6. Translated by Edna Worthley Underwood, in *Anthology of Mexican Poets from the Earliest Times to the Present Day* (Portland, Maine, 1932), pp. 152–54.

7. Translated by Dudley Fitts, in *An Anthology of Contemporary Latin American Poetry* (Norfolk, Conn., 1942), pp. 319–20.

8. Translated by Underwood, pp. 151–52.

9. Sonja Karsen, review of *Con palabras y fuego, Books Abroad* 38 (Spring, 1964), 177.

10. Gabriela Mistral, "Un poeta nuevo en América; Carlos Pellicer Cámara," *Repertorio Americano* 14 (1927), 373.

Chapter Four

1. Luis Rius, "*El material poético (1918–1961) de Carlos Pellicer,*" *Cuadernos Americanos* 124 (September–October, 1962), 248.

2. Translated by Mary and C. V. Wicker, in *Three Spanish American Poets: Pellicer, Neruda, Andrade* (Albuquerque, 1942), pp. 9–10.

3. Translated by Donald Justice, in *New Mexican Poetry,* ed. Mark Strand (New York, 1970), p. 173.

4. Andrew Debicki, "Perspective and Meaning in the Poetry of Carlos Pellicer," *Hispania* 56 (December, 1973), 1009.

5. "Hacia 1924, cuando ya triunfaba el Ultraísmo en América, Pellicer contribuyó—con *6, 7 poemas,* (1924)—no sólo a afirmar la metáfora y la imagen como la esencia virtual de la poesía, sino que abrió el camino para que los nuevos poetas de México otra vez instalaran en su predio nativo, en toda América, la confianza en las ofrendas de este Nuevo Mundo . . ." (Alfredo Roggiano, *En este aire de América* [Mexico City, 1966], p. 172).

Chapter Five

1. José González de Mendoza, "Hora y veinte con Carlos Pellicer," *Repertorio Americano* 20 (1930), 88, 95.

2. Luis Rius, "*El material poético* de Carlos Pellicer," *Cuadernos Americanos* 124 (September–October, 1962), 251.

3. Translated by Mary and C. V. Wicker, in *Three Spanish American Poets: Pellicer, Neruda, Andrade* (Albuquerque, 1942), pp. 12–13.

4. Andrew Debicki, "Perspective and Meaning in the Poetry of Carlos Pellicer," *Hispania* 56 (December, 1973), 1010.

5. Translated by Wicker, p. 15.

6. Cited in Laurette Séjourné, *Burning Water: Thought and Religion in Ancient Mexico* (New York, 1960), p. 142.

7. "Para Carlos Pellicer, como para Teófilo Gautier, el mundo exterior existe. Necesita ver, oír, oler, gustar, tocar. Ha logrado sus más brillantes aciertos cuando ha transcrito en sus poemas las agudas relaciones que su ojo aguileno percibe entre las cosas" (González de Mendoza, pp. 88, 95).

8. "El panteísmo de la poesía de Pellicer es civilizado, deportivo, sin drama interior, de bellos tonos plásticos" (Ortiz de Montellano, "Un camino de poesía," *Contemporáneos* 5 [September, 1929], 151).

9. "Arrebatos épicos, acentos griegos y plumas de Quetzalcoatl se mezclan con nidos de paloma en su mundo de artista primitivo y moderno" (Ibid., p. 151).

Chapter Six

1. "El poeta toma con la brillante hoz de su intuición los granos de oro del sustancioso y cósmico trigo poético" (Merlin H. Forster, "El concepto de la creación poética en la obra de Carlos Pellicer," *Comunidad* 4 [October, 1969], 687).

2. Concerning the four elements Pellicer later wrote *(La pintura mural de la Revolución Mexicana* [Mexico, 1960], p. 4): "We breathe air, we drink water, we cultivate the earth, we use fire. Among these four elemental forces, man has his existence. His power of will is the basis of all his activity. His natural and heroic impulse, for his own well-being, is to dominate the elements and obtain better production with less effort."

3. See E. M. Wilson, "The Four Elements in the Imagery of Calderón," *The Modern Language Review* 31 (January, 1936), 35–47.

4. Laurette Séjourné, *Burning Water: Thought and Religion in Ancient Mexico* (New York, 1960), p. 90.

5. Ibid., pp. 87–88.

6. Ibid., p. 94.

Chapter Seven

1. For a more detailed analysis of this poem see my article, "Motivos precolombinos en la poesía de Carlos Pellicer," *Explicación de Textos Literarios* 3 (1974), 51–57.

2. "Entrevista con Carlos Pellicer," in Pabón, "Gravitación de lo indígena en la poesía de Carlos Pellicer" p. 224.

3. The translation is that of Mary and C. V. Wicker, in *Three Spanish American Poets: Pellicer, Neruda, Andrade* (Albuquerque, 1942), p. 22.

4. Translation here appeared under the title, "Rhetoric of the Landscape," *Mexican Life* 8 (April, 1931), 15.

5. Carolyn Brandt Schlak, "The Poetry of Carlos Pellicer" (Ph.D. diss., University of Colorado, 1967), p. 20.

6. Review of *Exágonos, The Handbook of Latin American Studies* 7 (1941), 456–57.
7. Lloyd Mallan, "Five Mexican Poets." *Poetry* 61 (March, 1943), 682.
8. Translated by Wicker, p. 18.

Chapter Eight

1. "Por eso nos parece poco justo que se le siga motejando de poeta paisajista. Para él, poesía significa compentración de hombre con naturaleza. Una de las técnicas dominantes de toda su obra es la personificación de la naturaleza" (Frank Dauster, "Aspectos del paisaje en la poesía de Carlos Pellicer," in *Ensayos sobre poesía mexicana* [Mexico, 1963], p. 47).
2. Pabón, "Gravitación de lo indígena en la poesía de Carlos Pellicer," p. iii.
3. J. M. Cohen, "The Eagle and the Serpent," *The Southern Review* (April, 1965), 365.

Chapter Nine

1. "Yo siempre he hecho la diferencia que hay entre el poema y la poesía. Entonces este es un poema político en que a veces se filtra algo de poesía. Pero no considero que este poema sea, propiamente, un texto poético. Es un poema político. Cuando se hable de la poesía política pues a mí me da mucha risa. La poesía no es política. No puede ser. La política es una cosa tan transitoria. . . . Y la poesía es una fuerza misteriosa permanente" (quoted in George O. Melnykovich, "Reality and Expression in the poetry of Carlos Pellicer" [Ph.D. diss., University of Pittsburgh, 1973], p. 181).
2. "Este poema fue escrito para la ceremonia de rehabilitación de una parte de la zona arqueológica de Teotihuacán, y leído por su autor en dicho solemne acto celebrado ante la pirámide de la Luna la mañana del día 17 de Septiembre de 1964, con asistencia del entonces Presidente de los Estados Unidos Mexicanos, licenciado Adolfo López Mateos. Los últimos trece versos están dedicados al Presidente López Mateos y aluden a su obra extraordinaria de gobierno" (Pellicer, *Teotihucán, y 13 de agosto* [Mexico City, 1964], p. ix; all further references will be to this edition with the page numbers in the text).
3. "Como se puede ver, las imágenes están construídas en base de una estructura real y simbólica—los cinco puntos cardinales—que actúa como un eje invisible cuyo movimiento configura los contornos geométricos de la pirámide, desde la base horizontal hasta la idea del vértice" (Pavón, "Gravitación de lo indígena en la poesía de Carlos Pellicer," p. 139).
4. "En determinado momento el poeta se ubica dentro del contexto emotivo del poema y nos dice en cierta medida lo que está haciendo estéticamente en la obra" (Pavón, Ibid., p. 150).

5. Laurette Séjourné, *Burning Water: Thought and Religion in Ancient Mexico* (New York, 1960), pp. 109–10.

6. Pabón, p. 164.

7. Schlak, "The Poetry of Carlos Pellicer," p. 54.

8. "Estos pequeños poemas justifican mi pasión natal por todo lo cristiano. Creo en Cristo como Dios y la única realidad importante en la historia del planeta. Todo lo demás—arte, ciencia, etcétera—es accesorio, secundario y anecdótico. Desde siempre organizo 'El Nacimiento' cada Navidad en mi casa. Estoy seguro que es lo único notable que hago en mi vida. Es casi una obra maestra. He podido conjuntar la plástica, la música y el poema, así, cada año. Miles de gente van a mi casa durante cinco o seis semanas, un largo rato de noche a mirar 'El Nacimiento.' Los poemas que forman esta sección se escribieron siempre horas después de haber terminado mi trabajo anual.

"Mi madre, tan humana cuanto religiosa, me inició en la divina práctica de 'El Nacimiento.' Gracias a Dios y a ella, pude, puedo, hacer cada diciembre lo que dura un mes y parece eterno" *(Material poético,* p. 615).

Chapter Ten

1. Jorge Carrera Andrade, *Reflections on Spanish-American Poetry* (Albany, N.Y., 1973), p. 18.

2. "Si López Velarde y Tablada inician nuestra poesía contemporánea, Carlos Pellicer es el primer poeta realmente moderno que se da en México. No insurge contra el Modernismo: lo incorpora a la vanguardia, toma de esta y otras corrientes aquello útil para decir lo que quiere decir. Cuando muchos de los Contemporáneos exploraban los desiertos de la conciencia, Pellicer redescubrió la hermosura del mundo: el sol que arde sobre los ríos vegetales del trópico, el mar que a cada instante llega por vez primera a la playa. Sus palabras quieren reordenar la creación. Y en ese 'trópico entrañable' los elementos se concilian: la tierra, el aire, el agua, el fuego le permiten mirar 'en carne viva la belleza de Dios.' Mágica y en continua metamorfosis, su poesía no es razonamiento ni prédica: es canto" *(Poesía en movimiento* [Mexico City, 1966], p. 365).

3. "Más bien, él pertenece espiritualmente a esa generación que, guiada por el impulso de José Eustasio Rivera, se dedicó a describir la América Latina, avivada y conmovida por el instinto tropical" *(La poesía mexicana del siglo XX* [Mexico City, 1966], p. 34).

4. "Literature and Myth," in *Relations of Literary Study,* ed. James Thorpe (New York, 1967), p. 33.

5. See my essay, "Paz and Fuentes: How Close?" *Caribbean Review* 6 (April–June, 1974), 27–31.

6. Nicolás Guillén, *El son entero* (Buenos Aires, 1947), p. 34.

7. *Man-Making Words: Selected Poems of Nicolás Guillén,* trans. and

ed. Robert Márquez and David Arthur McMurray (Amherst, Mass., 1973), p. 143.

8. Ibid, p. 73.

9. "Introduction," in *Selected Poems of Pablo Neruda*, ed. and trans. Ben Belitt (New York, 1961), p. 19.

10. Ibid, pp. 148–49.

11. Ibid, p. 27.

12. *Neruda and Vallejo: Selected Poems*, ed. Robert Bly (Boston, 1971), p. 95.

13. Robert Bly, "The Lamb and the Pinecone: An Interview with Pablo Neruda," in *Neruda and Vallejo*, p. 158.

14. *Reflections on Spanish American Poetry*, p. 68.

15. "Introduction," in *Visitor of the Mist*, trans. G. R. Coulthard (London, 1950), p. 7.

16. Ibid, p. 58.

17. *Neruda and Vallejo*, p. 170.

Selected Bibliography

PRIMARY SOURCES

Colores en el mar y otros poemas. Mexico City: Librería Cultura, 1921.
Piedra de sacrificios, Poema iberoamericano. Mexico City: Editorial Nayarit S.A., 1924.
6, 7 poemas. Mexico City: Aztlán-Editores, 1924.
Bolívar. Mexico City: Secretaría de Educación Pública, 1925.
Hora y Veinte. Paris: Editorial París-América, 1927.
Camino. Paris: Talleres de Tipografía Solsona, 1929.
Esquemas para una oda tropical. Mexico City: Secretaría de Relaciones Exteriores, 1933.
Estrofas del mar marino. Mexico City: Imprenta Mundial, 1934.
Hora de junio. Mexico City: Ediciones Hipocampo, 1937.
"Ara virginum." Mexico City: *Revista de Literatura Mexicana* 1, no. 2 (October–December, 1940), 214–25.
Recinto y otras imágenes. Mexico City: Edición Tezontle, 1941.
Exágonos. Mexico City: Nueva Voz, 1941.
Subordinaciones: Poemas. Mexico City: Editorial Jus, 1949.
Práctica de vuelo. Mexico City: Colección Tezontle, 1956.
Museo de Tabasco, Guía Oficial. Mexico City: Instituto Nacional de Antropología e Historia, 1959.
Material poético, 1918–1961. Mexico City: Ediciones UNAM, 1962.
Con palabras y fuego. Mexico City: Fondo de Cultura Económica, 1962.
Teotihuacán, y 13 de agosto: ruina de Tenochtitlán. Mexico City: Ediciones Ecuador 000′0, 1964.
"Líneas por el Che Guevara." *Cuadernos Americanos* 22, no. 2 (March–April, 1968), 105.
Primera antología poética. Mexico City: Fondo de Cultura Económica, 1969.

SECONDARY SOURCES

1. Books and Dissertations
CARBALLO, EMMANUEL. *Diecinueve protagonistas de la literatura*

mexicana del siglo XX. Mexico City: Empresas Editoriales, 1965. Contains an important interview with Pellicer.

CUESTA, JORGE. *Antología de la poesía mexicana moderna*. Mexico City: Contemporáneos, 1928. Contains some brief but telling comments on Pellicer's early poetry.

DAUSTER, FRANK. *Ensayos sobre poesía mexicana*. Mexico City: Ediciones De Andrea, 1963. A collection of essays on various members of the *Contemporáneos* generation. Contains an excellent introductory essay on the generation itself and an important study on landscape in Pellicer.

GAMBOA, RUBÉN ANTONIO. "La poesía de Carlos Pellicer: Búsqueda de la consubstancialidad." Ph.D. dissertation, Tulane University, 1967. Studies concept of consubstantiality in poetry of Pellicer.

LEIVA, RAÚL. *Imagen de la poesía mexicana contemporánea*. Mexico City: Imprenta Universitaria, 1959. A highly impressionistic though useful essay on Pellicer.

MELNYKOVICH, GEORGE O. "Reality and Expression in the Poetry of Carlos Pellicer." Ph.D. dissertation, University of Pittsburgh, 1973. Studies Pellicer's relationship to vanguardism in general and Creationism in particular.

PABÓN, FRANCISCO. "Gravitación de lo indígena en la poesía de Carlos Pellicer." Ph.D. dissertation, Rutgers University, 1969. An excellent study of pre-Columbian motifs in Pellicer.

SCHLAK, CAROLYN BRANDT. "The Poetry of Carlos Pellicer." Ph.D. dissertation, University of Colorado, 1967. A general study of theme and technique in the poetry of Pellicer.

2. Articles

DE ANDREA, PEDRO F., and MELNYKOVICH, GEORGE. "Carlos Pellicer: Aportación bibliográfica." *Boletín de La Comunidad Latinoamericana de Escritores* 4 (June, 1969), 8–26. An annotated bibliography of works by and on Pellicer.

DEBICKI, ANDREW. "Perspective and Meaning in the poetry of Carlos Pellicer." *Hispania* 56 (December, 1973), 1007–13. Stylistic analysis of several important poems.

FORSTER, MERLIN H. "El concepto de la creación poética en la obra de Carlos Pellicer." *Comunidad* 4 (October, 1969), 684–88. A study of Pellicer's treatment of poetry as a theme.

LARA BARBA, OTHÓN. "Carlos Pellicer: Testimonios (Ensayo Biblio-iconográfico)." *Boletín del Instituto de Investigaciones Bibliográficas* 5 (January–June, 1971), 9–117. An extensive annotated bibliography of Pellicer.

MELNYKOVICH, GEORGE. "Carlos Pellicer and Creationism." *Latin American Literary Review* 2 (Spring–Summer 1974), 95–111. Highlights features of style in Pellicer's verse.

MULLEN, E. J. "Motivos precolombinos en la poesía de Carlos Pellicer." *Explicación de textos literarios* 3, no. 1 (1974), 51–57. Studies important pre-Columbian motifs in Pellicer's poetry.

ORTIZ DE MONTELLANO. "Un camino de poesía." *Contemporáneos* 5 (September, 1929), 150–52. An early reference to Pellicer's modernity.

PAZ, OCTAVIO. "La poesía de Carlos Pellicer." *Revista Mexicana de Literatura* 5 (May–June, 1965), 486–93. Stresses role of Pellicer as Mexico's first modern poet.

PUGA, MARIO. "Carlos Pellicer." *Universidad de México* 10 (February, 1956), 16–19. An interview with important biographical information.

RIUS, LUIS. "*El material poético* de Carlos Pellicer." *Revista Iberoamericana* 124 (September–October, 1962), 239–70. An extensive review of Pellicer's *Material*. Highlights major themes.

VILLAURRUTIA, XAVIER. "Cartas a Olivier." *Ulises* 1 (June, 1927), 13–17. An early discussion of the importance of Pellicer in Mexican literature.

3. Translations

FITTS, DUDLEY. *An Anthology of Contemporary Latin American Poetry.* 2d ed. Norfolk, Conn.: New Directions, 1947.

MALLAN, LLOYD et al. *Three Spanish American Poets: Pellicer, Neruda, Andrade.* Albuquerque: Swallow and Critchlow, 1942.

STRAND, MARK. *New Poetry of Mexico.* New York: E. P. Dutton, 1970.

UNDERWOOD, EDNA WORTHLEY. *Anthology of Mexican Poets from the Earliest Times to the Present Day.* Portland, Maine: Moser, 1932.

Index

Abreu Gómez, Ermilo, 21, 22
Alberti, Rafael, 30
Annals of Cuauhtitlan, 85
"América, no invoco tu nombre en vano"
    (Neruda), 149
Antena, 21, 22
Antología de la poesía mexicana moderna
    (Cuesta), 27, 46, 74
"El apellido" (Guillén), 146
Arciniegas, Germán, 28
Arrom, José Juan, 144
Ateneo de la Juventud, 20, 23
Ateneo de México, 16, 17, 20
Atenistas, 23
Avidez (Ortiz de Montellano), 47
Azuela, Mariano, 23, 26

Barreda, Gabino, 15, 20
Batista, Fulgencio, 124
Bly, Robert, 151
Bolívar, Simón, 29, 34, 43, 45, 51, 52,
    59, 82, 83, 111, 124, 126
Borges, Jorge Luis, 30
Braque, George, 34
Burgoa, Father, 103

Calderón de la Barca, Pedro, 91
Cámara de Pellicer, Deifilia, 19, 111, 136
"Un camino de poesía" (Ortiz de
    Montellano), 86
Campos, Rubén M., 19
"Canción de otoño en primavera"
    (Darío), 63
Canto general (Neruda), 149
"Caña" (Guillén), 145
Carballo, Emmanuel, 19, 32, 165–66

Carrera Andrade, Jorge, 46, 141, 144,
    145, 150–51
Caso, Alfonso, 17, 92
Caso, Antonio, 15, 16
Castillo Armas, Carlos, 124
Castillo Ledón, Luis, 16
Charlot, Jean, 25
Chávez, Carlos, 79, 101
Chichén-Itzá, 96
Chimborazo, el, 51
Científicos, 16
Clemente Orozco, José, 49, 134
Cohen, J. M., 122
Comte, Auguste, 15
Constitution of 1917, 15
Contemporáneos, 17, 18, 19, 20, 21, 22,
    24, 26, 28, 49, 74, 85, 86, 126, 141,
    147, 151
El corazón delirante (Torres Bodet), 47
Coulthard, G. R., 150
Cravioto, Alfonso, 16
Creationist theories, 46, 47, 98
Crisol, 22, 24
Crowley, Malcolm, 151
Cuadernos Hispanoamericanos, 28
Cuauhtémoc, 59, 60, 61, 111
Cuesta, Jorge, 21, 27, 94, 166

Dadaism, 26
Darío, Rubén, 16, 17, 30, 52, 63
Dauster, Frank N., 17, 28, 106, 144, 166
De Andrea, Pedro F., 28, 166
Debicki, Andrew, 75, 78, 79, 166
De la Selva, Salomón, 64
Delibes, Leo, 42
Destierro (Torres Bodet), 26

Díaz Dufoo, Carlos, 22
Díaz, Porfirio, 15
Díez Canedo, Enrique, 30

Empedocles, 90
Equatorial man, 83
Escuela de Altos Estudios, 20
Escuela Nacional Preparatoria, 19
Esquema generacional de las letras hispanoamericanas (Arrom), 144
Estrada, Genaro, 22
Eurindia (Rojas), 49

La Falange, 21, 22
Federation of Colombian Students, 28
Federation of Mexican Students, 28, 50
Fervor (Torres Bodet), 47
Fitts, Dudley, 167
Forster, Merlin H., 88, 166
Freyre, Ricardo Jaimes, 16
Frye, Northrop, 52, 142
Fuentes, Carlos, 135, 144
Futurism, 26

Gamboa, Rubén A., 106, 144, 166
García Lorca, Federico, 30
García Maroto, Gabriel, 25
García, Pardo, 141
Gastélum, Bernardo J., 21, 25
Gautier, Théofile, 86
"Generation of 1924," 144
"Generation of 1927," 30
Gervasio Artigas, José, 111
Gironella, Alberto, 138
Gladios, 20, 22, 32
Gómez, Juan Vicente, 50
Gómez Palacio, Martín, 20
Góngora y Argote, Luis, 27
González de Mendoza, José, 85
González Martínez, Enrique, 15, 17, 18, 20
González-Prada, Manuel, 16, 49
González Rojo, Enrique, 20, 21
González Salas, Carlos, 28
Gorostiza, Celestino, 26
Gorostiza, José, 20, 21
Grupo Minorista, 147
Guevara, Ernesto "Che," 126

Guillén, Nicolás, 126, 141, 144, 145–48
Guillén, Palma, 138
Gutiérrez Nájara, Manuel, 16
Guzmán, Martín Luis, 23

Haiku, 42, 46, 87
Handbook of Latin American Studies, 101
Haya de la Torre, Víctor Raúl, 62
Henríquez Ureña, Pedro, 16, 39
Hernández, Miguel, 30
Herrera y Reissig, Julio, 16
Hidalgo, Alberto, 47
Historia de Oaxaca (Burgoa), 103, 143
Hughes, Langston, 126
Huidobro, Vicente, 46, 47

Icazbalceta, García, 21
La ilustre familia (de la Selva), 64
Indianist novel, 144
Ingenieros, José, 29
Iturbe, Francisco, 29

Jaimes Freyre, Ricardo, 16
Jiménez, Juan Ramón, 30
Jiménez Rueda, Julio, 26
Júarez, Bénito, 15, 125

Kahlo, Frida, 138
Karsen, Sonja, 61

Lara Barba, Othón, 166
Larbaud, Valéry, 26
Latin American Congress of Writers, the, 30
"Law of the Center," 93, 96, 132
Leiva, Raúl, 166
Lerín, Manuel, 28
"Literature of the Revolution and Revolutionary Literature" (Ortiz de Montellano), 23
López Mateos, Adolfo, 30, 129, 132
López Velarde, Ramón, 17, 24, 33, 141
Lugones, Leopoldo, 16, 17
"La llave de fuego" (Carrera Andrade), 150
"Llegada" (Guillén), 146

Maestro, 29
La malhora (Azuela), 26
Mallan, Lloyd, 101, 167
Mallarmé, Stéphane, 27
Martí, José, 30, 51, 125
Martínez Peñaloso, Porfirio, 46
Martínez Ulloa, Enrique, 25
Marx, Karl, 152
Melynkovich, George, 28, 46, 47, 124, 166
El Mercurio, 66, 85
Mérida, Carlos, 25
Mexican Ministry of Foreign Relations, The, 94
Mexican Revolution, The, 15, 16, 22, 49
México Moderno, 20, 21, 22
Miccaotli, 92
Michoacán, the state, 64
Mistral, Gabriela, 30, 61, 66, 85, 106
Modernist period, The, 16, 142
Momotombo, el, 51
Monet, Claude, 34, 40, 41
Monguío, Luis, 149
Monsiváis, Carlos, 142
Montenegro, Roberto, 33
Monterde, Francisco, 21
Montezuma, 59
Morelos y Pavón, José María, 111
Motivos del son (Guillén), 145
Mullen, E. J., 160, 162, 167
Mysticism, 51, 55, 60, 121, 122, 127

Nahua-Aztec Culture:
    Art, 65, 92, 103, 134
    Artistic language, 110, 129
    Civilization, 49, 51, 52, 53, 61, 84, 90, 119, 133, 143
    Cosmology, 60, 92, 110, 134
    Culture, 92, 143
    Mythology and religion, 59, 60, 83, 86, 92, 93, 100, 103, 106, 108, 111, 129, 130, 144
    Symbolism, 53, 59, 61, 92, 93
Neruda, Pablo, 138, 145, 148–50
Nervo, Amado, 19
Nocturnos (Villaurrutia), 26
Nouvelle Revue Française, The, 21
Novo, Salvador, 18, 20, 21, 30, 47, 126

Oaxaca, 103
Obregón, Álvaro, 19
Ors, Eugenio, d', 30
Ortega y Gasset, José, 25
Ortiz de Montellano, Bernardo, 20, 21, 23, 24, 25, 26, 27, 47, 86, 167
Ortiz Rubio, Pascual, 29

Pabón, Francisco, 52, 53, 62, 106, 109, 129, 132, 135, 166
Pacheco, León, 25
"Palabras en el trópico" (Guillén), 147
Pan Americanism, 22, 49, 51, 62, 75, 106, 126
Pantheism, 57, 60, 86, 98, 106, 122
Parra del Riego, Carlos, 47
Paz, Octavio, 28, 84, 135, 142, 144, 167
Pellicer, Carlos: appraisal, 27, 30, 47–48 61–62, 74–76, 86, 87, 93, 99, 112, 122, 141–52; birth, 19; critical reactions to, 28, 45–47, 61–62, 63, 75, 77, 85–86, 88, 92, 93, 101, 106, 109, 128–29, 132, 134–35, 142, 144, 148, 149; earliest published verse, 20, 29, 32; early years and education, 16, 19–27; influence of López Velarde, 17–18, 24, 33; influence of Santos Chocano, 19; introduced to pre-Hispanic art, 18, 52–53, 65; relationship to Contemporáneos, 17, 20–28, 32, 46, 49, 141, 147, 151; views on Christianity, 33, 42, 58, 69, 81, 106, 114–17, 119–21, 122, 136
WRITINGS—POETRY:
"A Bolívar," 45
"A Cristo," 122
"A Germán Arciniegas," 58
"A Juárez," 123, 125
"A la poesía," 88, 104
"A Rufino Tamayo," 138
"El agua," 90
"Aire," 90
"Al dejar un alma," 74
"Al poeta colombiano Germán Pardo García," 104
"Aniversario," 69
"Apuntes coloridos," 37

"Aurora," 64–65, 66
Ara virginum, 112
"Ave María," 119
"Balada trágica del corazón," 59, 145
"La Bayadera," 42
"Brujas," 87
Camino, 27, 29, 32, 87–93, 118
"Canción de primavera,"
"Canto del amor perfecto," 69
"El canto del Ususmacinta," 108–111,
    127, 129, 143
"Canto destruido," 138
"Cien líneas para ti," 123, 124–25
Cinco poemas, 30
Colores en el mar y otros poemas, 29,
    32, 32–48, 51, 63, 64, 76, 77, 87,
    93, 135
Con palabras y fuego, 30, 59–61, 123,
    129, 135, 145, 149
"Confesión," 136
"Cosillas para el nacimiento," 137
"Cuba," 58
"Cuba divina," 145
"Dame, oh bosque," 74
"La danza del incensio," 42
"Deseos," 72–74, 76, 112, 137
"Discurso a Cananea," 123, 124
"Discurso por las flores," 107
"Divagación del puerto," 58, 145
"Domingo," 81
"Dos danzas de Tórtola Valencia," 42
"Elegía," 58, 70–71, 72, 76, 87, 145
"Elegía apasionada," 134
"Elegía ditirámbica," 82–83
"El encuentro," 89
"En Atenas," 84
"Envío," 92
"Esmaltín en la playa el cangrejo," 42
"Esquemas para una oda tropical," 30,
    94–98, 129, 132, 143, 150
"Estrofa neoyorquina," 87
"Las estrofas a José Martí," 123, 125
Estrofas del mar marino, 30
"Estudio," 39, 41, 42, 56, 77, 79–80,
    87, 92, 104
"Estudios," 84, 104, 105
"Estudios venecianos," 87
Exágonos, 30, 100–101

"Flora solar," 135
"Fragmentos," 89
"El fuego," 90
"Grecia," 32
"Grupos de palomas," 77–79
"He olvidado mí nombre," 138–40,
    146
"Historia," 58, 145
"La hora de David," 87
Hora y veinte, 29, 77–86, 92
Hora de junio, 30, 32, 94–100, 101,
    137
"Horas de junio," 99–100
"Iguazú," 56, 57
"Invitación al paisaje," 98, 99
"Líneas por el Che Guevara," 123,
    125–26
"Lutos por Antonio Mercé," 104
"El mar Jónico," 87
"Mater Admirabilis," 119
"Mater Amabilis," 119
Material poético, 28, 30, 123, 137, 138
"Mira como se van esas nubes de
    otoño," 38
"Motivos," 66
"La muerte," 92
"La nieve," 57
"La noche," 68, 69
"Noche sin sombra," 38
"Nocturno," 32, 69, 71, 74, 117
"Nocturno a mi madre," 111, 112
"Oda," 51–52, 56
"Oda a Cuauhtémoc," 59–61, 123,
    142, 146
"Oda al sol de París," 83
Otras imágenes, 103–105
"Otros Sonetos," 120
"Paisaje," 81
Palomas, 30
"París, canción de primavera," 83
Piedra de sacrificios, 29, 30, 49–62,
    63, 70, 71, 74, 75, 78, 98, 111, 123,
    145
"Poema elemental," 89–93, 95, 109,
    132
"Poema en tiempo vegetal," 60, 108
"Poema pródigo," 98
"Poética del paisaje," 98

Práctica de vuelo, 30, 112–22, 123, 136
"Primavera," 64
Primera antología poética, 28
Recinto, 101–103
Recinto y otras imágenes, 30, 32, 101, 106
"El recuerdo," 81
"Recuerdos," 137
"Recuerdos de Iza," 43, 44, 87
"Recuerdos de los Andes," 43
"Regina caeli," 119–20
"Retórica del paisaje," 98–99
"Romance de Tilantongo," 103, 143
"Ruego," 81
"Sandalía de espuma saqué del océano," 42
"Scherzo," 66, 74–75, 76
"Segador," 66–67, 88, 103
Seis, seite poemas, 18, 29, 32, 63–76, 77, 88, 103, 112, 137
"Semana holandesa," 80–81
"Sembrador," 66–68, 87, 103
"Siete sonetos para Gabriela Mistral," 138
"El sol," 34, 41
"Soledades," 68–69
"Soneto a causa de me tercer viaje a Palestina," 112
"Sonetos bajo el signo de la cruz," 113, 115
"Sonetos de la esperanza," 115
"Sonetos de la luz," 115
"Sonetos de otoño," 103
"Sonetos dolorosos," 112, 120
"Sonetos fraternales," 118–119
"Sonetos lamentables," 114
"Sonetos nocturnos," 116–18
"Sonetos para el altar de La Virgin," 119
"Sonetos romanos," 20, 32
"Sonetos suplicantes," 115
"Sonetos todo un día," 115, 117
Subordinaciones, 30, 60, 106–12
"Suite brasilera: poemas aéreos," 56, 98
"Surgente fin," 123, 126–29, 130, 143
"Tema para un nocturno," 111, 112
"Tempestad y calma en honor de

Morelos," 111
Teotihuacán y 13 de agosto: Ruina de Tenochtitlán, 30, 123, 129–35, 143, 146
"La tierra," 91, 93
"Toda América nuestra," 123, 125
"Uxmal," 52–56, 90, 104, 109, 116, 127, 129, 135, 139, 143
"Variaciones sobre un tema de viaje," 81
"Viernes," 80
"La voz," 32, 98
Pérez Jiménez, Marcos, 124
Poesía en movimiento (Paz), 141
La poesía mexicana del siglo XX (Monsiváis), 142
Poetry, 101
Pongs, Hermann, 128
Popocatépetl, el, 51
Popular Alliance for American Revolution, The, 62
Posdata (Paz), 144
Positivism, 15
Puga, Mario, 167

Queremel, Ángel Miguel, 47
Quetzalcoatl, 83, 85, 92, 96, 104, 110, 130, 131, 133, 143
Quincunx, 93, 95, 143

Ramos, Samuel, 21, 22, 25
La raza cósmica (Vasconcelos), 50, 51, 52
Reflections on Spanish-American Poetry (Carrera Andrade), 141, 150
Reflejos (Villaurrutia), 48
Rembrandt, Van Rijn, 40, 41, 80
Repertorio Americano, 66
Residencia en la tierra I & II (Neruda), 138, 148
Revista de Avance, 147
Revista de Occidente, 21
Revista de Revistas, 85
Revueltas, José, 30
Reyes, Alfonso, 16, 17
Rius, Luis, 39, 46, 63, 167
Rivera, Diego, 25, 49, 104, 138

Rivera, José Eustasio, 142
Roggiano, Alfredo, 76
Rojas Pinilla, Gustavo, 124
Rojas, Ricardo, 49
Romano Muñoz, josé, 22

Sabines, Jaime, 110
Saint John of the Cross, 121
Salazar Mallén, Rubén, 26
San-Ev-Ank, 20, 22
Santos Chocano, José, 16, 17, 19, 59
Sarmiento, Domingo Faustino, 51
Savia Moderna, 16
Schlak, Carolyn, 100, 135, 144, 166
Séjourné, Laurette, 92, 134
Sierra, Justo, 111
Siqueiros, David Alfaro, 49
El soldado desconocido (de la Selva), 64
Somoza, Anastasio, 124, 125
Sóngoro cosongo (Guillén), 145
Spanish Civil War, 126, 145
Spencer, Herbert, 15
Stabb, Martin, 16
Strand, Mark, 167
Straub, William J., 46
Sueños (Ortiz de Montellano), 26
Surrealism, 26

Tablada, José Juan, 17, 42, 100, 141
Tamayo, Rufino, 34
Taracena, Alfonso, 45
Times Literary Supplement, The, 28
Todos los gatos son pardos (Fuentes), 144
Toltec civilization, 133

Torres Bodet, Jaime, 17, 18, 20, 21, 24, 25, 26, 27, 28, 47
Torres Ríoseco, Arturo, 16
Tropical Town and Other Poems (de la Selva), 64
Trujillo, Rafael Leónidas, 124, 125
"Tuércele el cuello al cisne" (González Martínez), 15

Ulises, 21, 22, 27
Ultraism, 76
The Underdogs (Azuela), 23, 26
Underwood, Edna Worthley, 27, 167
Usumacinta, el., 51, 109
Urbina, Luis G., 19

Valery, Paul, 27
Valle-Inclán, Ramón del, 30
Vanguardism, 22, 76, 80, 81, 141, 142, 151
Vasconcelos, José, 16, 17, 29, 32, 49, 50, 51, 52, 61, 66, 83, 127, 134
Velasco, José María, 18
Verdadera historia de la Revolución Mexicana (Taracenà), 45
Vermeer, Jan, 80
Veinte poemas (Novo), 47
Villaseñor, Eduardo, 104
Villaurrutia, Xavier, 17, 18, 21, 26, 27, 32, 47, 48, 116, 126, 167

West Indies Ltd. (Guillén), 145

Xochipilli, 107